"CAN IT REALLY BE DONE?"

Money® magazine says it can—you *can* retire young and rich, if you know the answers to the most important questions about investing for retirement today:

- How much of my retirement fund should be in the stock market?
- How do I protect myself against a bear market?
- How do I figure out how much I need?
- Are tax-free, tax-deferred, or taxed investments the best for me now?
- What's the best age for me to retire?
- Where are the best places to live in retirement?

HOW TO RETIRE YOUNG  CH

Other books in the
Money® America's Financial Advisor series:

401(k) Take Charge of Your Future

Paying for Your Child's College Education

How to Retire Young and Rich

Joseph S. Coyle

WARNER BOOKS

A Time Warner Company

A NOTE FROM THE PUBLISHER

Copyright © 1996 by MONEY magazine
All rights reserved.

Warner Books, Inc., 1271 Avenue of the Americas, New York, NY 10020

 A Time Warner Company

Printed in the United States of America
First Printing: February 1996
10 9 8 7 6

Library of Congress Cataloging-in-Publication Data

Coyle, Joseph S.
    How to retire young and rich / Joseph S. Coyle.
      p. cm.
    Includes index.
    ISBN 0-446-67164-9
      1. Retirement—Planning. 2. Retirement income—Planning.
I. Title.
HQ1062.C69 1996
646.7'9—dc20   95-43177
                                     CIP

Cover design by Bernadette Evangelist
Cover illustration by Peter Hoey
Book design by Giorgetta Bell McRee

ACKNOWLEDGMENTS

This book draws primarily on my seventeen years of work as a **MONEY** magazine writer and editor—specifically on the three **MONEY** guides and dozens of articles I have edited on retirement planning. For most of those projects, my "top editor" was Frank B. Merrick, assistant managing editor of **MONEY** magazine, to whom I owe special thanks for his knowing guidance, unerring judgment, and pitiless pencil. I also wish to thank the following experts for being valued sources for some of the information on which this book is based: Helen Dennis, for the "How Ready Are You?" retirement quiz; Peter A. Dickinson, Norman Ford, Alan Fox, John Howells, Saralee Rosenberg, David Savageau, and Robert Tillman for helping determine the 20 top places to retire; Seymour Goldberg for expertise on IRA distributions; Richard Krueger and Jane Parker for insights on retiring abroad; and Paul Westbrook for generously sharing his knowledge and thinking on all areas of retirement planning.

The Retirement Worksheet on page 38 is adapted for this book from the "How to Retire Rich" seminar system by special arrangement with the Personal Finance Network, Moss Adams, Seattle, Washington 206-223-1820.

CONTENTS

Introduction   ix

CHAPTER   1
Four Things You Need to Do Now   1

CHAPTER   2
What's the Right Age to Retire, Anyway?   12

CHAPTER   3
What to Do about Social Security   22

CHAPTER   4
The Key: How Much You Will Need   30

CHAPTER   5
How to Evaluate a Buyout   41

CHAPTER   6
How to Invest for Your Future   47

CONTENTS

CHAPTER 7
How to Choose Mutual Funds 62

CHAPTER 8
Getting the Most out of Savings Plans 74

CHAPTER 9
Getting the Right Kind of Help 81

CHAPTER 10
The Spoiler: Health Care 95

CHAPTER 11
How to Choose Your New Hometown 102

CHAPTER 12
The Ultimate Fantasy: Retiring Abroad 121

CHAPTER 13
How to Handle the Biggest Wad You'll Ever Own 126

CHAPTER 14
The Lowdown on Variable Annuities 137

CHAPTER 15
How to Keep from Outliving Your Money 144

CHAPTER 16
Five Years to Go: 10 Things to Do 159

CHAPTER 17
Six Months to Go: Nine Things to Do 170

Index 177

INTRODUCTION

Young people planning their retirement? Twenty- and thirtywhatzits plotting out their pensions? At first the idea sounds morbid, a bit like designing your headstone. But poll after opinion poll in recent years has come up with the same conclusion: Saving enough for retirement has become one of the two or three top preoccupations among American adults of all ages.

Just think about it for a minute, and it makes perfect sense. Retirement used to be that last brief stage of life. Social Security and a small pension would see most people through it just fine. Now look at retirement: 30 years, maybe half of them in robust health—maybe all of them, the way medical science is advancing.

What we have before us is nothing less than a second chance at life, the opportunity to start all over again—older, of course, but wiser and not a lot worse for wear. Early retirement, you say? Show that to your grandparents and they'd see it for what it really is: two lives instead of one. But not, alas, two lives for the *price* of one. And there's the rub. People are leaving their jobs earlier and living longer. And they know instinctively, even those fresh from college, that it's going to take a heap of cash to get you through your second lifetime. Thus the issue becomes both a lasting joy and an early sorrow. It's wonderful to know that life will be healthy and long. But the polls also reveal that most people fear they will never be able to accumulate enough to retire early *and* to pay for it all.

And they're right. Most of them won't have enough saved up by the time they're ready to call it quits. And many will take the leap anyway, only to go broke halfway through their golden years. But you? Will you be one of the clever minority who succeed in retiring young and rich enough to live comfortably well into your nineties?

First here's the answer you expect: Read this book and you'll find out how to do it. The younger you are, the better your chance of retiring young and rich. But even if you are within a few years of retirement, you should not give up. Just as retirement has spread out to encompass three decades, young and rich have altered their meanings as well. If you are able to retire at 45, say, you may have four decades or more to look forward to. By any standard, that's young. And the new definition of rich is even simpler to grasp: having enough to see you through to the end of a long, active life.

Now for a glimpse of grim reality, based on long experience: mine as a personal finance writer and editor for the past 17 years; and the accumulated wisdom of dozens of retirement planners I have interviewed. The message is this: Even when confronted with the irrefutable truth, the one and only path to financial security, most people fail to carry through with what they ought to do. Being only human, they resist at some level of their intelligence the two or three searing lessons they should never forget. They dawdle. They worry. They deny, telling themselves that they don't have the money we say they need to do it anyway. All of this takes time, and the longer you wait, the harder it becomes to build your minifortune.

So out of deep respect for human weakness, I want to introduce right now the four concepts that have to get hammered deep into your psyche so that you will see the challenge with such blinding clarity that you will be radicalized and will *act*. These four ideas are not new; you may know them well. What you may not realize is that they undergird all of the strategies that will be unfolding later on in this book. That's why this quartet will be reappearing over and over again, why you need to feel their presence at every turn, and why they are taking a bow right here.

• Inflation: the unstoppable tide that washes away your savings. Next to plain stupidity, inflation is nature's greatest impediment to building a superior nest egg and keeping it from running out. Always must be taken into account as you plan ahead.

• Growth Investments: the ones that do best over time and the only ones that consistently beat inflation. Primarily stocks and stock mutual funds.

• Compound Interest: alias the miracle of compounding. The marvelous mushrooming effect created by the interest you earn on principal plus the interest you earned earlier on that same principal, and so on. Income that compounds on a tax-deferred basis is the best. For instance, $10,000 compounding at a rate of 8% a year inside a tax-deferred IRA would grow to $21,600 in 10 years, $46,600 in 20 years, and $100,627 in 30 years.

• Aloneness: also known as "You're on your own." The

daddy and mommy who used to do it all for us, tucking us comfily into our later years, have both run out of money and, if truth be told, out of concern for us. Those financial parents are Uncle Sam, with his Social Security benefits, and our employer, who used to put all the money we needed into our pensions and just hand them over to us on retirement. Uncle Sam now sees Social Security as an entitlement, and an entitlement is something that has to be cut. If you're young now, write off at least half of what your parents are expecting (or getting) from Social Security. And those traditional pensions have turned into monstrous money eaters. They're being replaced by newfangled pensions called 401(k)s and such. But they don't pay you as much as the old ones did. Besides, who stays around a company long enough to build up a real pension anyway? So now you really need that 401(k). But you also need to save and invest on your own. Once you had two caring money parents. Now you're a semi-orphan. But you've got a plan. And here it is. . . .

CHAPTER 1

Four Things You Need to Do Now

To retire young and rich. If you could see it, it would probably be a beach. If you could smell it, it would be rum, limes, and suntan lotion. If you could hear it, what else? The surf. This fantasy may be the most shopworn cliché of all—the eternal vacation. But it symbolizes one of the deepest of human yearnings—freedom. What it doesn't do is get you closer to the reality. In fact, the fantasy can turn into an opiate, unless you figure out the way to turn the dream into a well-focused goal. And to do that you will have to rearrange some of the furniture in your life. For example, you almost certainly will need to figure out a way to spend less so you can save more. Sounds like a drag, and undoubtedly it will be uncomfortable at first. But it's that old unavoidable: reality. And yes, you ought to do it soon. Now is best.

This chapter is about the handful of things that you should do as soon as possible. You have to understand that

1

these are not your odd assortment of on-the-fridge don't-forget-to-do's, the kind of directions that no normal, busy, happily flawed human ever really follows—like "Clean out at least one closet every month." They are much more important than that. In fact, they will serve as the foundation of your dream. In time they will turn your dream into a plan with a built-in safety net. So take these four strategies to heart as seriously as though you were signing a contract for life. Indeed, to work, that's what they have to be.

1. Learn to Save More Than You Ever Dreamed You Could.

Here's why this rule is the most basic of all. As stated in the introduction to this book, the savers and investors of this world are now largely on their own. Social Security and pensions together will not be enough to carry you through your longer life. You will need to open your retirement drive on a third front—your own savings.

As you will see when you figure out how much you will need to retire (covered in Chapter 4), your own savings may need to be substantial to cover a long postwork period. For instance, let's say your household income at retirement is $80,000 a year. You even wait until you're 65 to call it quits. Financial planners use a rule of thumb that people on average will need 80% of their pre-retirement income to maintain the same living standard later on. And say you estimate you will live 20 more years and that the inflation rate will average 4% a year over that time. How much will you need? A cool $1.17 million. If you figure to live 30 more years—and many planners say it's wise to make that assumption to be sure your money doesn't run out before you do—you will need $2.18 million.

2

That's the demand side of the picture. You will need lots of money for your long later life. Very challenging. Now let's take a look at the supply side: you. Also very challenging, because of the widespread belief among middle-class Americans that trying to save is futile. It's hard all right, but it isn't futile. Here's why:

We live in a hyperconsumer economy. More than economy, really: it's a consumer culture, bred in the bone and impossible to escape unless you quit society entirely and live alone in the desert. This culture knows not the face of self-denial. It has forgotten the concept of postponed pleasures upon which middle-class life was built. So you must accept the proposition that you are deeply affected by this culture, that you are really part of it. Then you must realize that when someone says "I just can't save a cent," that person really believes what he or she is saying. Then you must learn to resist a knee-jerk agreement and a supportive "That's right!" Instead, at least to yourself, you must substitute a skeptical "Let's look at the record."

The record is abysmal from any point of view. The United States sports one of the lowest savings rates in the world, far lower than that of many poorer countries. The low-savings mind-set starts early, when mere tots become raving consumers as they absorb hour after hour of TV commercials. By the time these consumers are in the workforce themselves, they are beaten down by the widely accepted notion that young people today cannot possibly achieve the wealth their parents amassed. For example, people in the fifties and sixties bought their homes before the great real estate inflation of the 1970s and 1980s, and many are wealthy just on the gain they have made on their houses. By contrast, people in their twenties, thirties, and forties by and large have had to buy in at inflated rates. All true. It's also true that the cost of a college education, which has

3

raced ahead of inflation for decades, is the other big reason why today's workers are having a hard time making ends meet, much less saving for their retirement.

In short, saving is far from easy. But as previously noted, two powerful forces are at work to make the problem seem unsolvable—perception and superficial reality. The perception is the sense of powerlessness fueled by the strongest desire to consume ever known to humankind; the reality is the higher cost of everything we consume, starting with housing and education.

Yet ask any expert on credit or financial planning and you'll be told that the bottom-line reality is something quite different: Unless you are truly poor, there is always some "give" in your budget, something that can be cut far short of the bone. One frivolous image comes to mind: all the young folk who consume several $3 caffe lattes each day while complaining that they'll never be able to afford to buy a home of their own. Should they deny themselves the pleasure of good coffee? Not necessarily. It's just that today's superconsumers have holes in their jeans they don't even know are there. What they have surely never done is figure out how much those holes are costing them, how much a home would cost them, comparing the two sides of the ledger, and then making an informed decision about what really matters to them most.

So if retiring young and rich appeals to you, or even if you're more motivated by not retiring old and poor, you will have to save regularly. And the amount you'll have to save will probably be a lot more than you now save or think you can manage. You'll see how much when you get to Chapter 4. For the time being, let's follow the consensus advice of financial experts who say that from your thirties on—that is, once you get settled in your career with expectations of regular raises as well as increasing expenses—you should be aiming to save at least 10% of your pretax income. You make $50,000 a year? If you're not saving at least $5,000 of that, you're falling behind. And you know what that means: If you start saving in earnest sometime later on, you may have to hike that percentage to 20% or more to make up not only for the savings you didn't stash, but for the investment returns you didn't get along the way.

Here, then, without undue tedium or slogging are the basics on how to save regularly.

First of all, take a Saturday afternoon and sit down with your checkbook and a record of your credit-card charges for the past 12 months. Segregate all your bills by category for the last 12 months. Then tot up each category. At the end you will see how many dollars you spent over the past year on housing, utilities, eating out, travel, clothing, and so on. Unless you are an unusually astute bookkeeper, the results should surprise you—some of the results, that is. You will begin to get a sense of just where you have been overspending and, thereby, just where you will be able to cut back in order to beef up your savings.

To help you zero in on the culprit categories, here is a general estimate of the ideal range for each. There are two sets here—one for young singles in their twenties and one for couples in their forties with two incomes and two children.

	Singles	Couples with Two Kids
Housing	20–25%	30%
Loan payments	13–15%	13–15%
Food	10–15%	10–15%

Child care	0%	8–10%
Entertainment	7–14%	3–7%
Vacations	3–7%	3–7%
Pocket money	8–12%	5–8%
Transportation	7–10%	7–10%
Clothing, personal care	4–8%	4–10%
Education	5–7%	5–7%
Utilities	4–7%	4–7%
Contributions	2–7%	2–5%
Savings	5–10%	10%
Insurance	1–3%	3–5%

You should also try to make your savings automatic, wherever possible. That way there won't be any of those poignant struggles with yourself over the tragedy of self-denial. If it doesn't go through your hands, you won't miss it. At least you won't miss it the way you would if you had to part with it painfully every month. Your first automatic savings vehicle should be your company savings plan, because of the tax savings and, often, the matching dollars tossed in by your employer. (More on that later.) Many corporations also make regular payroll deductions and put the proceeds into a bank account or mutual fund for you. Alternatively, automatic transfers can be made from your checking account each month to your mutual fund company.

You can also use the "pay yourself first" approach. Simply make sure that your retirement savings are among the first of the bills you pay each month. This may require an enormous change in the way you or your spouse think about saving. For instance, many financially sophisticated people nevertheless believe that the only way to handle their accounts is to pay down all of their debts before saving anything. As long as you have credit-card obligations outstanding, for instance, nothing goes for retirement.

This is a grievous error in thinking because it robs you of those twin dynamos that make your savings grow so amazingly—growth stocks and compound interest. For example, if you set out to save $1 million by the time you're 65, assuming an average annual return of 7%, here's how dramatically your contributions and the actual earnings of your savings would vary depending on when you begin. If you start saving at 35 and therefore have 30 years to save, you will have to put $820 a month into your account. At the end of the 30 years, your contributions will amount to $300,000; the other $700,000 will come from the investment earnings. But if you start at 60, with only five years to save, you will have to put in $13,870 a month and $840,000 of your own hard-earned, after-tax dollars; only $16,000 will come from investment return.

Another technique is to commit your next raise to savings. The easiest way to do this, of course, is to call your company payroll department and have the raise put into your employee savings plan. You can also promise yourself that any windfalls that come your way—from a tax refund to a spot bonus to an inheritance—will go into your savings.

2. Max out on Your 401(k) or Other Tax-Deferred Retirement Plan.

If you're making headway with strategy number one, number two will be easy. That's because you will be saving enough to be able to put the maximum amount of dollars into your tax-deferred plan. If you work at a company that offers a 401(k) plan to employees, grab it. This should be where your first savings dollars go. Only when you have put as much as possible into your 401(k) should you go on to other ways to invest. What else not only defers taxes while your money is working, but does it on a before-tax basis?

Yet even that isn't what really makes 401(k)s so central to getting richer younger. The twin pistons powering these savings vehicles are taxes, taxes, taxes, and compounding, compounding, compounding. Together, tax deferral and compounding make dollars multiply as nothing else can do. Here is an astounding illustration: Take a 35-year-old who earns $60,000 a year and puts 6% of his salary into a taxable investment that earns 8% a year. By age 65 he would have accumulated a total of $185,744 after paying taxes at a rate of 30%. By contrast, if he were to take that same amount of money and put it into a tax-deferred account like a 401(k) or an IRA, his pile would have grown to more than double the taxed amount—to a lofty $407,820 when he reached 65.

You can improve even on that if your employer matched your 401(k) contribution, as some 85% of them do. Typical match is 50 cents on the dollar, up to a certain percentage of salary, usually 6%. The employee can usually put in up to 10% of his or her salary, to a limit of $9,240 in 1995.

Other tax-advantaged plans that may be appropriate for you:

• IRAs. You can put as much as $2,000 of your compensation ($2,500 if one spouse is employed) into an IRA. But if you are already enrolled in a company plan, you can fully deduct your IRA contribution only if you earn less than $25,000 (for singles) or $40,000 (for married couples filing jointly). If you and your spouse are part of no company plan, you can take the full deduction. So IRAs are best for those who have no company plans.

• 403(b)s. Similar to 401(k)s, these are for employees of schools and charitable organizations.

• SEPs. These are best for self-employed people who are the sole proprietors of their business; contributions are restricted to the lesser of $22,500 or 13.04% of annual compensation.

• Keoghs. These are terrific ways for small-business owners funding plans for themselves and their employees to stash big hunks of income in tax-deferred accounts. They're complicated and sophisticated, so anyone ready to take one on may need help from an accountant.

• Annuities. These come in two varieties, variable and fixed. They're best for people who have put the maximum into other tax-deferred plans. (See Chapter 14 for more on annuities.)

3. Never Endanger Your Principal: In Other Words, Be an Investment Realist, Neither Too Risk-Prone nor Too Risk-Averse.

To retire young and rich, even if you start saving in your twenties, even if you put most of your money in growth stocks, even if you max out on your tax-favored plans at work—in short, even if you follow all the textbook do's and don'ts—you may still not accumulate enough savings in time if you aren't clear on the issue of risk. What it comes down to is simple: You will want to sensitize yourself gradually to almost instinctively taking the right amount of risk. Then your investments will grow fast, but not so fast that they burn out.

All this sounds ludicrously obvious. In theory that is true.

But in practice many investors become obsessed with fear, put all their money into 5% bank CDs, and watch from behind their triple-locked doors as their returns over the years are consumed entirely by inflation.

On the other hand, many other investors are inflamed by greed, often whipped to this frenzy by even greedier stockbrokers who get them to put their money into super-risky investments that flame out and leave nothing behind. This path is far more damaging than the meek and fearful route. At least there you are left with your principal. But when you lose big, you have to win double big to make up. In fact, one of the first things investment pros learn is that if you lose 50% of your money, you have to make up 100% just to break even. Getting into that predicament makes you either give up and retreat to the safety of CDs or redouble your risk and set yourself up for a greater fall the next time.

The sensitizing process mentioned is especially delicate for people at either extreme of the risk spectrum: too timorous or too daring. As you absorb Chapter 6, "How to Invest for Your Future," you'll see this need for balancing risk take on concrete form.

4. Put a Safety Net under Your Earning Capacity.

The last foundation factor that is absolutely essential to achieving your goal is your steadily improving income. This also may seem resoundingly obvious. But in today's economy it is far from it. Hundreds of thousands of professionals and managers in their forties and fifties have been let go by downsizing companies in recent years. Their stories are by now familiar to any newspaper or magazine reader or TV news watcher. These people by and large walked out into a completely different job climate from the one that prevailed when they last were looking for work. After years of trying, many of them had to face the bitter reality that they would never again be employed at the same high rate of pay. Many had to settle for far lesser jobs. And many more entered a kind of enforced early retirement. For such people, retirement planning and saving stopped dead the day their downsizing companies let them go. Their future looks bleak as they slowly but surely run out of money.

So it is just good common sense and prudent insurance of future security for today's employees to have an escape hatch from a career that is about to be cut off. However, this is not a book about careers; dozens of other books tackle the great contemporary issue of job security. If you haven't already plotted out your escape from job death, search out one or more of these books and don't rest until you have figured out how to keep your income high and assured until you retire.

A final note: Knowing where and how you can jump if your job self-destructs is a useful exercise for after retirement, too. For many reasons both emotional and financial, more and more retirees work. With 30 or so more years to look forward to, why not? This pungent subject is discussed in Chapter 15, "How to Keep from Outliving Your Money."

CHAPTER 2

What's the Right Age to Retire, Anyway?

This chapter is not about your finances. It is the only one in this book that isn't. Instead it's about your emotional readiness to stop working. If your immediate reaction is to skip to the next chapter, try to resist, because the issue at hand is crucial. It is, in fact, the dark underside of retirement planning that tends to slip and slither past the hard dollars-and-cents numbers of saving and investing. It is important because without taking a hard accounting of your emotions, you are apt to drift into a long retirement of misery and boredom. Thousands are doing it every day.

Let's be very specific. You're interested in early retirement or you wouldn't be reading this book in the first place. If you retire early at, say, 60, you will be looking at around 30 years of leisure. If you call it quits at 50, it's 40 golden ones. And if you do everything so right that you can knock off at 40, you will be looking down the vastness of a half century of postwork life. Money aside, it stands to reason that you can't just rock and rock and rock through three or four decades of unrelieved torpor, especially when you are apt to be starting out on that journey in excellent health and full of zip. A far cry from the condition of retirement back in 1935, when Social Security was born: you could start getting your benefits when you were 65 all right, but the average life expectancy for the American male back then was just 63.

You have to recognize the fact that the whole meaning of retirement has changed. It used to consist of a few years of exhausted old age. Period. Now it's decades of healthy seniority, what has come to be called the new third quarter. Throughout history, life was divided into thirds: youth, middle age, and old age. But stupendous advances in medicine have substituted a four-part setup: the first quarter (growing up and being educated); the second quarter (work); the third quarter (continued work or retirement or a combination of both); and the fourth quarter (old age, largely leisure, but some work as well if you can and want to). The third quarter is a historical innovation that no one was prepared for because no one had experienced it before this generation.

Great advances like the third quarter—or early retirement, if you prefer—don't just happen. They cause some dislocation along the way. In this case, the tension-producing question is, How do you reconcile getting out early with living to 90? That, in fact, may be the lifestyle question of the next century, as the great baby boom generation takes rock and roll, instead of the rocking chair, into their golden years. Bottom line? There is no single one, actually, but a choice among three: (1) Retire early and keep busy; (2) Retire gradually; or (3) Keep on truckin'.

Finding out which is for you is a crucial exercise in ensuring your future emotional security. While most people know at some level if they're not saving enough for retirement, research and polls repeatedly indicate that finding the age that is right for you to retire is not so easy to fathom. Besides an element of denial, there is also more than a little blissful ignorance involved.

Just think: What is retirement? A kind of prolonged vacation, right? And what experience do you have with this kind of life? Why, your summer vacations, of course. And how long are they? Two weeks? Three weeks? Four weeks if you're really lucky? Retirement planners report that roughly six months after their clients stop working, the vacation phase ends and reality sets in. In short, they get tired of being on vacation and get bored.

Roughly a quarter of these new retirees, according to surveys, report that they are unhappy, largely because they have discovered too late that they were not ready to retire in the first place.

Testing Your Readiness to Quit

In a minute you'll run into a simple-to-complete, 14-step quiz that will help you find out if you are ready to retire. As you'll see, it probes your feelings about your job, your spouse, yourself, your friends, and the future. It won't be hard for you to figure out how all these points get at your emotional preparedness for a life of unaccustomed freedom. What you may not figure out right away is that those points all boil down to two basic questions:

1. Is your mind already detaching from your workplace or are you just as in love with your job as you ever were?

2. Have you begun to see retirement as an adventure or is it a vague, somewhat frightening prospect?

Studies of retirees find that most of them really wanted to retire and only a minority felt that they were pushed. Reasons why people wanted to go range from healthy ones like wanting to move on to something new, including both work and leisure activities; to less happy ones like poor health or a feeling of being underappreciated or hounded by unyielding stress.

Often these negative reasons for wanting to retire are precursors of equally grim states of mind after you quit. Experts on the subject preach the gospel of positive thinking and the discipline of flexibility. But how do you build these traits, particularly if you tend to be rigid and afraid of change?

You begin by attending a retirement-planning seminar. About a quarter of large employers run free comprehensive seminars for their employees, and nearly three out of four offer some kind of retirement counseling. If this avenue doesn't work for you, or if you are too young to avail yourself of it, try writing to the American Association of Retired Persons (at 601 E Street N.W., Washington, D.C. 20049) and requesting information about retirement planning. Since early retirement is so attractive and accessible to those who really want it, you should start testing your emotional readiness at least a decade before you think you might want to retire. This way you are forced out of the realm of pure unchallenged fantasy. And if you're lucky, you'll confront your own buried feelings about work and not working.

You can test yourself on just that issue right now. In fact, by taking the following quick quiz, designed by Helen Dennis, a retirement specialist at the University of Southern

California in Los Angeles, you can begin to gauge roughly how far away you are from being ready to call it quits. (One caution: The test is aimed at people who have been working for at least 20 years. Younger workers will find, for example, that youth alone makes them more assured of the long-term availability of jobs.)

HOW READY ARE YOU?

Check all the answers that apply to you.

1. The feeling that I make a difference at work is
   a. extremely important to me.
   b. somewhat important to me.
   c. of little importance to me.
   d. not at all important to me.

2. My co-workers and colleagues
   a. are like my family.
   b. are my major social contacts.
   c. are rarely seen by me (and my spouse) outside work.
   d. are not very important to me.

3. At work, I feel
   a. energized.
   b. extremely important.
   c. underutilized.
   d. overworked and underpaid.

4. To meet my financial obligations and responsibilities, I am counting on
   a. my next pay raise.
   b. increasing my savings.
   c. winning the lottery.
   d. my spouse.

5. Retirement means
   a. you're over the hill.
   b. you haven't yet peaked.
   c. you are old.
   d. you have new choices.

6. Power and influence are
   a. aspects of my work that I thoroughly enjoy.
   b. an essential aspect of my work.
   c. not characteristics that apply to me.
   d. almost impossible to achieve in retirement.

7. I plan to retire and live
   a. alone.
   b. with my spouse.
   c. with a friend.
   d. with my mother.

8. I feel
   a. attractive.
   b. unattractive.
   c. vigorous.
   d. mentally sharp.

9. I currently have
   a. some wonderful hobbies.

    b. at least one volunteer commitment.

    c. few outside interests.

    d. some outside interests I would like to develop.

10. **My spouse (or significant other)**

    a. is eager for me to retire.

    b. dreads my retirement.

    c. has my chores planned.

    d. has packed our bags for a trip.

11. **I consider myself**

    a. a good self-manager.

    b. a planner.

    c. a procrastinator.

    d. one who can advise others but has difficulty taking my own advice.

12. **Knowing I will have free time in retirement,**

    a. I have planned how I will use my time.

    b. I don't have a clue what I will do.

    c. I have a plan, but I don't know if it will be fulfilling.

    d. I think that I am already overcommitted.

13. **Most of my friends**

    a. are working and plan to continue working.

    b. are retired.

    c. plan to retire soon.

    d. are split among all of the above.

14. **I recently have thought about**

    a. the losses I might feel when I retire.

    b. how my spouse and I will get along in retirement.

    c. what gives meaning to my life.

    d. none of the above.

Score: Give yourself one point for checking each of the following items: 1a, 2a, 2b, 3a, 3b, 4a, 4b, 5a, 5c, 6a, 6b, 6d, 7a, 8b, 9c, 10b, 11c, 11d, 12b, 12c, 13a, 14d. The higher the score, the less emotionally ready you are for early retirement. Here are some general interpretations of your score:

15 to 22 points: Either early retirement is not right for you or you need to start preparing emotionally for it immediately.

9 to 14 points: You are a possible candidate for early retirement but need a little more emotional preparation.

8 points or fewer: Don't give this issue another thought; you can retire happily tomorrow.

The Third Way: Work after Work

What if, after probing your feelings honestly, you decide that retirement is not for you, at least not now? Let's say that, like many other Americans, your very identity is bound up with what you do for a living. And most of your friendships revolve around the office. And you are afraid you have saved too little and would be terrified to retire with that threat hanging over you. And you never developed any outside interests or hobbies.

In that case there is no question: Don't think about retiring now. But do think about getting yourself ready for at least a slowdown from your present pace before too long. Do be forearmed with outside friends and interests, if only for the reason that your early retirement may not be your decision. Diversification is absolutely essential in investing, as you will see in a later chapter of this book. But it's also indispensable in your larger life.

But what if you find yourself in a much more familiar state of mind and heart over retiring—you want to cut back gradually, but not all at once? In short, you want to work part of the time. Be assured about one thing:

You will be far from alone. Roughly half of all retirees work at least part-time. That proportion is expected to grow significantly in the coming decades as baby boomers enter their later years, many of them unprepared financially for the leap to leisure. And as corporations and government continue to downsize, armies of consultants and temporary workers—many of them executives and professionals—are coming onto the scene. In addition, many companies are finding that older workers have experience and commitment to work that make them highly prized part-timers.

Whether you work for pay or not, it is far from the only alternative to plain, unalloyed leisure. Two others are already major presences in the lives of retirees and are destined to grow: going back to school for the pure pleasure of it, and giving your time to others for the deep satisfaction it brings.

Pursuing college courses has become a second career for retirees and a huge new market for universities. Many people love the experience so much, they virtually become itinerant scholars, journeying from campus to campus both here and abroad, taking courses for small fees, and living a charmed life in the process. The Elderhostel Program (75 Federal St., Boston, Mass. 02110; 617-426-8056) has a free catalog of such far-flung offerings. If you want just to study, not to wander, call up the colleges in your area.

Volunteering is another growth industry, for two reasons. As the ranks of the retired swell, more and more young retirees who don't need to work for pay will be looking for ways to make themselves useful. Second, as government trims away at its budgets, more and more of the work of social service agencies will be done by charitable institutions and their legions of volunteers. The real secret of volunteering is that doing for others takes volunteers out of themselves and gives them unexpected joy. Some people find volunteer work a revelation—more rewarding than all the jobs they ever did before.

CHAPTER 3

What to Do about Social Security

It's become unquestioned dogma among experts on personal finance that your retirement fund, to be adequate, must draw on three main sources: your company plans, your own individual savings and investments, and Social Security. The problem with this scenario is that hardly anybody believes it.

Just look at a recent national study by Equitable Life of affluent baby boomers, pre-retirees, and retirees. All three groups agreed that their company plans are their single most important retirement income source: 48% of boomers, 43% of pre-retirees, and 40% of retirees voted for company plans. Next came individual investments, which got the nod from 18% of boomers, 23% of pre-retirees, and 15% of retirees. What about Social Security? It landed in last place generally. But its showing was so low as to be ignominious: only 2% of boomers, 3% of pre-retirees, and 14% of retirees voted Social Security their single most important income source.

True, these are affluent people: the median income of the boomers in the survey is $84,000 a year, $93,000 for the pre-retirees. But their biases are typical, and you'll find them expressed in any recent poll on the subject. The most famous instance is the survey revealing that more adults under the age of 34 believe in UFOs than think they'll get any Social Security at all. It is practically a given in boomer thinking that by the time they retire, Social Security won't be around to take care of them. And with the first boomers destined to turn 55 in 2001, and presumably start their early exodus from the workforce around then, it won't be very long before we see if their gloomy outlook is correct.

Well, is it? Emphatically, no. Social Security will continue to be an important element of retirement income for most Americans as far as the eye can see into the next century. Right now, in fact, it is far more generous a contributor to retirement finances than most people realize. For instance, the maximum benefit available to a 65-year-old in 1995 was about $14,500 a year. If that person's spouse was the same age and also entitled to the maximum benefit—a pretty typical case in a two-professional household—the couple would be receiving $29,000 a year, partially tax-free, from that source alone. They would have needed an investment portfolio worth $350,000 to produce that much income, assuming a return of 8%.

If that doesn't impress you, the cost-of-living factor might. Unlike your pension, which almost always stays petrified at the same amount for as long as you live, your Social Security benefit rises with inflation, lately about 3% or so a year. So that $14,500 a year that a 65-year-old received in 1995 would grow by about $3,000 in just six years. Hence, a couple with the same benefits would be getting $35,000 a year together by 2001. And at 3% a year, any benefit would double in around 24 years.

Because Social Security is such an emotional and political issue, it is useful to stop a minute and look at where we are.

Unless Congress does a 180-degree turnaround, Social Security will remain a supersensitive political issue that no politician would dare tackle. But everyone knows that something has to be done about Social Security before it wrecks the federal budget. The Social Security trust fund is slated to begin running deficits in 2013. That's when the first boomers turn 67. Between 2010 and 2030, the army of Social Security beneficiaries will grow by about a half, adding 26 million more people to the rolls. But the number of workers supporting the system will stay just about flat, a perfect recipe for disaster.

The best guess available is that Congress will somehow not be stupid enough to allow this mountainous problem to grow too big before doing something about it. Then benefits would take draconian cuts and disaster would have arrived. So look for fixes to be applied sometime within the next decade. They will consist of a combination of (1) increased taxes on benefits (today as much as 85% of benefits may be taxed, depending on your income); (2) further raising of the retirement age (it's scheduled to begin moving up from 65 to 67 in the year 2003); and (3) lowering of the cost-of-living allowance, which lately has been adding 3% or so a year to checks.

The crucial point is that none of these moves, alone or in combination, will destroy Social Security as we know it. Much of the sense of coming doom has been issuing from two sources, both of which are studded with conflicts of interest. The first is politicians of both major parties, who have made a practice of charging that their opponents are scheming to cut Social Security benefits. Often the accusations have no substance. No wonder Social Security has been called the third rail of politics: touch it and you die.

The second source of confusion is financial planners (for more on planners, see Chapter 9). If a planner can project little or no income from Social Security for a client, that means the client has to save and invest more to make up for the shortfall. And that helps a planner's case if he or she is earning fat commissions by selling annuities, mutual funds, or other financial products.

So let's get serious about what you can look forward to and how to ensure you get what you're entitled to.

The first thing to do is get a formal readout of your work history and projected benefits from the Social Security Administration. All you have to do is to call the SSA at 800-772-1213 and ask for a projection of your annual benefit. A few weeks later you'll get a detailed report stating the approximate size of your benefit-to-be, based on your income history and an estimate of how much you'll make between the present and your retirement. If you're 55 or older, in fact, the SSA already should be sending you an automatic annual report of your benefit projections.

Getting this accounting is important for two reasons. First, you will be better able to correct any errors of omission the SSA might have made on your record. While such mistakes are not common, the chances of their occurring have increased with the accelerated job-hopping that has become part of our work culture. Second, you will be able to figure out how much you need (coming up in the next chapter) much more accurately.

How Your Age Matters

Age has its privileges, an old rule that has new meaning when it comes to Social Security benefits. The older you are, the better off you are. The rundown starting with those who will be the most affected:

• **Born in 1960 or later.** You'll get the biggest hit. The generations who have enjoyed Social Security benefits from the outset in 1935 have by and large taken out of the system far more than they put in. For you, it will be the reverse. A worker who retired in 1980, by one estimate, received $63,000 more in Social Security benefits than he put in (calculated in 1985 dollars). You, on the other hand, will likely be allowed to keep only half of your projected benefit. On top of that, those born in 1960 or later will face a normal retirement age of 67 instead of 65; and early retirement at 62, which brings 80% of full benefit today, will bring only 70%.

• **Born between 1938 and 1959.** You'll feel some pain, but not a serious amount. For instance, those born in 1950 will see their normal retirement age rise to 66, from today's 65. The figure increases slightly each year until the year 2027, when it hits 67 years for those born in 1960. And early retirement at age 62 will bring 75% of the full Social Security benefit, down from 80% now.

• **Born before 1938.** Your benefits are safe, and you won't have to deal with any of the pushing back of the normal retirement age. However, you should expect to feel an increasing tax burden on your benefit check. Currently 50% of your benefits are taxed when your "provisional" income (that's adjusted gross income plus tax-exempt interest and half of your Social Security benefits) exceeds $35,000 on a joint return ($25,000 for a single). And when your provisional income runs over $44,000 on a joint return ($34,000 if you're single), up to 85% of your benefit is subject to federal income tax. You should expect that this trend toward taxing more and more of your Social Security benefit will continue. It would be wise to expect that if your retirement income is more than $50,000 or $60,000 a year, you'll pay income tax on most if not all of your Social Security.

When You Should Start

If you retire early, you can choose when to start taking your Social Security benefits. As you now know, waiting gets you more and waiting longer gets you even more. Sometimes it's wise to wait, sometimes it isn't. A rundown of your options:

• **Start at 62.** This means you'll spend the rest of your life collecting only 80% of what you might have gotten had you just waited three years. But on the other hand, it will take a long time even at a full benefit to make up for the three years of checks you might have been collecting. Perhaps the best way to decide is to look at how you will be financing the early years of your retirement. If giving up those Social Security checks between 62 and 65 means drawing on your investments, then you are probably better off taking the checks right away and leaving your portfolio intact, particularly if it's in growth investments with potential for big returns.

• **Start at 65.** If you have other sources of income that

make it unnecessary to draw on your investments, then it would be a good idea to put off Social Security until 65. Also, if you think you will be reentering the job market from time to time, as many early retirees do, that would be a strong reason for putting off your Social Security checks. Under 65, you lose $1 of Social Security benefits for every $2 of earned income above $8,160. If you're between 65 and 69, the bite is reduced slightly to $1 of benefits for every $3 you earn above $11,280.

• **Start at 70.** This can mean a big difference in your check because it goes up a bit for every single month you delay starting past age 65. Lately the amount has been an additional 4.5% a year, but it nearly doubles to 8% in the year 2008 and thereafter. That would increase a monthly check by more than 25% over the normal retire-at-65 rate. You should think about delaying until 70 if you plan to have earned income during much of your sixties despite retirement or if you come from a long-lived family. Remember also that the higher your benefit, the higher your spouse's survivor benefit after you die.

Which brings up our last Social Security discussion:

How You Qualify

You can become eligible for Social Security benefits in one of five ways:

1. With your own benefits, based on your lifetime work record
2. With spousal benefits, based on your husband's or

wife's work record (normally half of the spouse's full benefit)

3. With divorced spouse's benefit (providing you were married at least 10 years, your former spouse is receiving Social Security or is more than 62 years old, you are not remarried, and you have been divorced for at least two years)

4. With widow's or widower's benefits (providing you were married at least nine months and did not remarry before you turned 60)

5. With divorced widow's or widower's benefits (providing you were married to your ex-husband or ex-wife at least 10 years, are 60 or older, and married your present spouse before age 60)

CHAPTER 4

The Key: How Much You Will Need

Even if you invest like a lion and have the impression you're doing fine for the long run, not knowing just where you stand until you are ready to retire is a world-class catastrophe in the making. If you wait until the end and then do your calculations, what if you find out only then that you're 30% short of your requirements? There's simply not enough time to make up for such a shortfall. And don't kid yourself: More people wind up their careers with too little than with too much.

There is another important reason for knowing as early as possible how much you need to save. It's the psychological factor: Knowing exactly what your goals are means you'll know when you're not meeting them. And if you truly believe in a goal like early retirement, guilt over letting yourself down might—just might—get you to cut back your spending to bring your saving up to where it should be.

So whatever age you are, if you haven't figured out how much you need to save, now is the time to do so. If you're close to retirement, it's vital you find out now to determine how ready you are to stop receiving a paycheck. On the other hand, let's say you are in your early twenties, just starting out, making a modest entry-level wage, single, and totally enthusiastic about (1) retiring early and (2) an Armani suit, a Mazda Miata, and two weeks in the Greek islands. By knowing the trade-offs, you are much likelier to go for (1) and forgo most or all of (2). And the simple facts are these: If you are 35 years from retirement, by starting now and saving 10% of your income each year, you can expect to accumulate enough by the end of your career to retire. That's assuming you get a 9% annual gain on your money and inflation runs 3% a year. But if you wait just 10 more years and start saving when you are 25 years away from leaving work, you'll have to put away something like 21% of your pay.

Don't try using the above rule of thumb to figure your own needs, though. It's too rough, and the individual variables can change the numbers substantially. Instead, take a few minutes to fill out at least one of the two worksheets we provide in this chapter.

To make your job as simple as possible, in fact, you can skip the first worksheet—"What You'll Spend When You Retire"—if you like. This is where you get to estimate what percentage of your pre-retirement income you will need to live on after you stop working. It's a worthwhile exercise because younger retirees almost always spend considerably more than older, less mobile ones. Besides, the younger ones vary widely in their spending, from roughly 50% of pre-retirement pay for those who stay close to home and putter in the garden to 120% for those who live out the travel adventures they have been dreaming of for a lifetime.

If you decide to leave this worksheet blank, however, just use the rule of thumb many planners employ: You'll need 80% of your pre-retirement pay in retirement.

Before we start with the worksheets, there is another way to get this job accomplished: inexpensive, easy-to-use software. This might be the way to go if you own a computer and know the basics of using it. A section at the very end of this chapter discusses the computer alternative.

What You'll Spend When You Retire

This, as we noted above, is optional but highly recommended. In the "Current" column, enter the amounts you now spend each year on all the expenditures listed on lines 1 to 15. Unless you carry heavy credit-card balances, the total should equal your current income. Then estimate what your expenditures would be if you were newly retired ("Early Retirement" column) and then retired but over 75 years of age ("Late Retirement" column). Use today's dollars; the second worksheet takes inflation into account.

Here are simple guidelines for filling out each line of this worksheet:

Line 1. Housing will probably cost you just as much as it does now. Most retirees stay put in the same house, so they face the same property taxes and costs of homeowners insurance, utilities, and repairs. If you figure your mortgage will be paid off by then, or that you will be moving to a smaller house in a less expensive setting, take that into consideration. On the other hand, many retirees go from owning one home to taking on the responsibilities for two. If it's too early to decide on such matters, it's safe simply to assume that your post-retirement housing costs will be the same as your pre-retirement ones.

Line 2: Food costs are a major variable in retirees' budgets. That is because you can easily cut 25% from your food bill by not paying for your lunch at work five times a week. On the other hand, many retirees find that eating out becomes a major form of entertainment. Even counting early-bird specials and other discounts, restaurant meals almost always cost far more than eating at home. One way to predict your behavior after retirement is to gauge your enthusiasm for eating out now. If you are already a devoted restaurantgoer, figure that you will be even more committed to the practice when you have more time. In that case you might want to add 10% to 25% to your present bill when filling in line 2.

Line 3: Transportation costs will go down. You can subtract your commuting bill from your current account and maybe even a car if you now operate more than one.

Line 4: Taxes could represent your biggest saving of all, particularly if you don't work after you retire. First, you won't be paying the 7.65% Social Security and Medicare tax on wages anymore. Besides that, you might qualify for the exemptions some states allow on taxation of Social Security benefits and pensions. In general, though, as time goes on it is wise to expect these breaks to get rarer as budget-cutting federal and state governments look for more sources of revenue. Just recall how up to 85% of retirees' Social Security benefits are currently federally taxable, depending on income.

Line 5: Medical and dental expenses will most likely alter dramatically. If your employer is now paying for almost everything, you'll probably have to figure on a big new expense if you retire too early for Medicare to kick in at 65. Coverage for a married couple, for instance, can run to $6,000 a year. While no one can know precisely what their medical expenses will be, it's safe to assume that the older you get, the more attention you'll need. Experts advise that to cover yourself generally, you should add 25% to 30% to your pre-retirement medical expenses.

Line 6: Clothing and personal care items. You can figure on cutting this bill by 30% or 40% if you are leaving a formal office setting and entering a world of jeans and sweats.

Lines 7 and 8: Recreation, hobbies, and travel costs can both go up so much after retirement that they may threaten to wipe out most of your other economies. More and more, early retirement is a time of intense travel and recreation. But later retirement usually is a time of quiet and very modest travel and recreational activities.

Line 9: Education. The earlier you retire, the heavier the load might be in this area, since many early retirees have college-age children. If you will be lucky enough to be past that by then, you still might want to add an amount to cover your own course-taking, a fast-growing activity for seniors.

Line 10: Support of relatives may be nothing or it may be thousands of dollars if you have to pay for the care of your aged parents or if you decide to help your kids buy a house or pay for *their* kids' education.

Line 11: Loan and credit-card payments should be next to nonexistent when you retire. Any serious debt should be paid down before you stop working.

Line 12: Life and disability insurance. Life insurance costs should be less after you retire, and disability insurance should be unnecessary when you no longer have wages to protect.

Line 13: Savings and investments, contrary to what many people think, should not end with retirement. Since this is the principal way of combatting inflation, and you have to expect to be exposed to inflation for 30 years or more, experts recommend that you plan to save 5% to 10% of your income annually during the first decade or so of retirement.

Line 14: Gifts and contributions. It makes great sense financially and emotionally to cut back on your cash donations to charities after retirement and substitute volunteering.

Expenditure	Current	Early Retirement	Late Retirement
1. **Housing** (rent, mortgage, utilities, property taxes, upkeep, furnishings, homeowners insurance premiums)	_____	_____	_____
2. **Food** (includes alcohol and tobacco)	_____	_____	_____
3. **Transportation** (includes car loan payments, insurance, gas, repairs, parking, and commuting costs	_____	_____	_____
4. **Taxes** (don't include Social Security taxes after you retire unless you expect to work)	_____	_____	_____
5. **Medical and dental** (include insurance premiums, out-of-pocket expenses, prescriptions, and glasses)	_____	_____	_____
6. **Clothing and personal care items**	_____	_____	_____

7. **Recreation and hobbies** _____ _____ _____
8. **Travel** _____ _____ _____
9. **Education** (include savings for your child's education) _____ _____ _____
10. **Support of relatives** _____ _____ _____
11. **Loan and credit-card payments** _____ _____ _____
12. **Life and disability insurance** _____ _____ _____
13. **Savings and investments** _____ _____ _____
14. **Gifts and contributions** _____ _____ _____
15. **Other** _____ _____ _____
Total Expenditures _____ _____ _____
% of Today's Income <u>100%</u> _____ _____
Needed (divide total expenditures by your current income and multiply the result by 100)

How Much You Must Save

Once you have estimated what percentage of your pre-retirement income you will need after you retire, you can turn to the worksheet of worksheets, the one small but indispensable chore that will point you on the road to financial independence. This one will determine how much you need to set aside each year to reach your ultimate goal.

To fill out the entire nine lines of the worksheet, you will need estimates of both Social Security benefits you expect to receive after you turn 62 and any company pensions you may be vested in. (Today's early retirees collect 80% of their full benefits if they start getting their checks at age 62; the full amount kicks in if you start receiving checks at 65. But the 80% figure drops to 75% in 2005 and to 70% in 2022 as the age for full benefits rises from the current 65 to 67.) While the Social Security Administration will make a projection for you, it may not be so easy to get a fix on your pension payout if you are not within a decade or so of retirement. In any case, your employer's benefits department may be willing to make a projection if you ask. If not, you can do some rough calculations on your own. Figure that your pension will replace about 30% of your final pre-retirement pay, based on your years of service to the company and the average of your salary over the three to five highest-paying years on the job. Your company may have a simplified formula you can use to do your calculation.

When you finish the worksheet, you will almost certainly find that your Social Security benefit and your pension together do not cover your retirement income needs. They may have been enough once, but not anymore, thanks to the long, active retirements most people can expect. The shortfall is the challenge presented to you by this worksheet. You have to save and invest enough to make up that gap. The faster you do so, the earlier you can retire.

A couple of points before you start. We have adapted the worksheet from a retirement education program called "How to Retire Rich," which was developed by the Seattle accounting firm of Moss Adams. The worksheet assumes that you will live to 92, 10 years more than the current 17-year life expectancy for a 65-year-old. Other assumptions: (1) Your retirement account will grow 7% a year, based on historical averages for a conservative mix of stocks and bonds; and (2) Inflation will run 5% a year, in keeping with the average for the past three decades. Finally, you should recalculate this worksheet every two years or so to account for any changes in your retirement plans, your investment performance, and any changes in Social Security or your pension.

1. **Annual income needed at retirement** (Insert the average amount of current income required in early and late retirement from the previous worksheet or use 80% of your current income.) _____

2. **Estimated Social Security and pension** (Call Social Security at 800-772-1213 for a projection of your annual benefit. Ask your employer's benefits office to estimate your annual pension in today's dollars. Enter the total of both here.) _____

3. **Annual retirement income needed from savings and investments** (line 1 minus line 2) _____

4. **What you must save by retirement** (line 3 times factor A below) _____

5. **What you've already saved** (total of A, B, and C below)
   A. IRAs, SEPs, and Keoghs
   B. Vested amounts in employer savings plan
   C. All other investments _____

6. **Projected value of your current savings at retirement** (line 5 times factor B below) _____

7. **Total retirement capital you need to accumulate** (line 4 minus line 6) _____

8. **Annual savings needed to reach your goal** (line 7 times factor C below) _____

9. **What you must save each year until retirement** (line 8 minus the amounts you expect your employer to contribute annually to your company savings plans) _____

Age at retirement:
55 56 57 58 59 60 61 62 63 64 65

Factor A:
23.3 22.9 22.6 22.2 21.8 21.4 21.0 20.5 20.1 19.6 19.2

Years to retirement:
1 3 6 9 12 15 20 25 30

Factor B:
1.03 1.09 1.18 1.29 1.40 1.53 1.76 2.02 2.33

Factor C:
1.000 0.324 0.155 0.099 0.071 0.054 0.038 0.028 0.022

Source: The Personal Finance Network, Moss Adams, Seattle, Washington. Used by permission.

Or Try Some Easy-to-Use Software

You can forgo the worksheets in this chapter and even have a little fun in the process by letting a computer program figure out how much you will need to save each year for your retirement. Besides being easy and inexpensive, the software that can do the job guides you carefully through some exercises that will wind up giving you insights into financial planning that you otherwise might not get.

Three of the top mutual fund companies offer versions of retirement planning software that you can buy simply by calling an 800 number. There is no great difference among the three, which are for IBM-PC or compatible hardware, but you'll probably get the most out of Vanguard's Retirement Planner (800-876-1840; $17.50). The other two are Fidelity's Retirement Planning Thinkware (800-457-1768; $17.50) and T. Rowe Price Retirement Planning Kit (800-541-1472; $15.00).

Here's an idea of how the Vanguard software works. First it takes you through what's called a **savings planner**—different scenarios on the amount of income you may need for the term of your retirement. You can fool around with rates of return on your investments, inflation rates, the number of years you will live after you stop work, and so on. You can see quickly just when your money would run out in different scenarios and how much more you would need to save to make up the difference.

This program automatically computes your Social Security benefits and shows you how much your checks would shrink if you took early retirement. While the software also has a section that aims to help you with your investment planning, it's not much more than an introduction to the subject. The savings planner is the real gem and is well worth the price of admission.

CHAPTER 5

How to Evaluate a
Buyout

Hundreds of thousands of corporate employees have received those tantalizing and frightening offers in recent years: Give up your job and get a package of rewards in return. As both corporate and government downsizing continues, hundreds of thousands more will have to entertain buyout bids in the coming years. Depending on your situation and the size and quality of the offer that may come your way, accepting could be the answer to all your retirement dreams or the worst move in your financial lifetime.

The first thing to consider is the timing of such an offer in the context of your income-producing career. If a great offer comes just a few years before you were going to retire anyway, fine. But what if you're tempted with a buyout 10 or 20 years before you're ready to call it quits? Then you have to look beyond the glittering gift to whether you can find a job that pays as well as the one you're giving up.

For more and more "RIFfed" (for "reduction in force")

employees, the terrifying truth is that if you're over 40, you may never be able to replace the pay you're getting now. It's true that the growing army of temporary professional and management workers often earn as much as or more than staff people, but they get not a cent of benefits—no retirement accounts, no health care coverage. After all, the value of benefits can add the equivalent of a third or more to your compensation.

Another fact of life these days: Buyouts are getting skimpier. In fact, the downsizing of early-out offers themselves is used by companies as an incentive to get people to take the current buyout or face a smaller one the next time. Experts estimate that those most likely to face buyouts are employees over 55 who are in a shrinking business like retailing or defense. Such people have about a one-in-four chance of having to deal with such an offer.

Early out vs. Voluntary Separation

There are actually two types of buyout, and the first (the early-retirement offer) is usually a lot more generous than the second (the voluntary-separation package).

Early-retirement offers typically are aimed at employees who are 50 years of age or older. Many include a generous plumping up of pensions. For example, your employer may add from two to five years to your age or length of service or both in computing your traditional defined-benefit pension. (Your 401(k) is another matter.) So-called five-and-five offers—adding five years to your age and to your service)—were common in the 1980s, when companies were far more generous than they have become since. Today two-and-

42

two deals are more the standard. And it's likely that this will seem wildly generous in a few years from now.

Another common feature of early-out offers is bridging (in which a company adds an amount to your pension), say, from 60 to 62, roughly equivalent to the amount you will begin receiving from Social Security when you reach 62. This has the effect of having Social Security kick in at 60. Alas, it is also being axed by corporations looking to cut expenses. So if you're planning on retiring a decade or more from now, it might be wise not to count on a bridge even if your employer currently offers one. A general word of caution: Since early retirement packages are by far the more expensive form of buyout and are subject to complex government antidiscrimination rules, compensation experts predict that they will be seen less and less in the future.

Voluntary-separation deals, in effect, are already becoming the standard form of buyout. These can range from a pittance to a princely sum, but as with everything corporate these days, don't let your expectations run wild. The standard lately has been one to three weeks' salary for each year of service, often cutting off at one year's pay. Here's how to size up this type of offer: two weeks, reasonable; three weeks, excellent; and that rare offer of four weeks, solid gold.

Health insurance is an issue here for employees too young to be considered early retirees. In that case a good deal might be a year's continued health coverage. But many voluntary-separation offers end your health coverage as soon as you leave the payroll. Under federal law, however, you are entitled to stay on in your employer's medical plan for 18 months at your own expense. After that you'll have to look for private coverage until you are old enough to qualify for Medicare at 65. And if you're over 50, individual insurance could cost you $5,000 a year. Also, be careful if you live in a state where insurers can turn you down if you are not as physically fit as they require.

Making the Tough Choice

If you're closing in on retirement, even a not-so-good buyout offer may be worth taking. This is particularly true if the value of the buyout is about equal to the amount of pay you would make by staying on that extra year or two.

But what if you're years away from retirement? Then any offer—and not just a generous one—will require careful, even shrewd, consideration. Your first question should be, Does management *want* me to take this offer? While no one is forcing you to accept it, turning it down could lead you to wish you had taken it. The company could follow up with a period of harassment, demotion, pay cuts, even job elimination. To head off this hell, look for signs that may tell you whether you're wanted or not.

The best indicator is your boss. Does he appear happy with your performance—not over the long term, but your recent performance? If his attitude toward you appears to have grown negative in any way, you may have to connect that with the buyout and conclude that you are expected to leave. Also find out, if possible, whether the buyout is aimed at a specific department or job title. If that includes you, perhaps you should think about saying yes to the offer. You will likely have only two or three months to think the offer over, so make the best of that time.

What, then, if you are pretty sure you are not one of those targeted for the door, but the offer may be too generous to pass up? That's when you need to look beyond this job and determine whether you really can afford to let go of it. After all, your employer wants you to stay. So the next question is: How far will the buyout plus my other assets take me? If the answer is not nearly far enough to cover the rest of your life, you then have to take a hard look at your employment prospects. If the job outlook is healthy or you have realistic plans to set up your own business, you may want to grab the offer even if it is not the most generous you've ever heard of.

One more thing to think about is the bigger pension you would get if you stayed on at your present job. Study the table that follows, which demonstrates the dramatic differences between taking a buyout at 55 and staying on with the pension clock ticking until 65. Our example is a 55-year-old earning $50,000 a year with 20 years' service for a company. The buyout offer adds five years to both his age and years of service. That yields a pension the worker would not normally receive until he turned 60. He also gets an extra $6,800 for seven years as a bridge to Social Security, which kicks in at age 62 and pays a third more than the bridge stipend.

You can see in the table that by turning down the buyout and working until 60 or 62, the employee would raise his retirement income by as much as $8,891 a year. That's $6,891 in additional pension, $1,600 from his heftier 401(k), and $400 from his bigger Social Security check.

Age	Income with Retirement at 55 without the Package	Income with Retirement at 55 with the Package	Income with Retirement at Age 60	Income with Retirement at Age 62
55	$9,703	$21,177	$51,500	$51,500
60	9,073	21,177	17,354	59,700
62	19,273	24,577	27,754	33,468
65	19,273	24,577	27,754	33,468

Note: The table assumes that the employee's pension is based on his five highest years of earnings, that he gets 3% annual pay raises, and that he contributes 3% of his salary to his 401(k), which he annuitizes at retirement. Social Security kicks in at 62. *Source:* Kwasha Lipton.

What, then, is an employee determined to retire young and rich to do if a reasonable buyout offer comes along? The smartest strategy is to be prepared by having the next step in your career all plotted out. Do you have live leads to your next job if it comes to that? Or do you have realistic prospects for starting your own business? If not, you may be in no position to take the money and run. And that would be a shame if the offer is a tempting one.

CHAPTER 6

How to Invest for Your Future

Here is where you'll really be put to the test. Up to this point, basically you've been asked to do two things: (1) make sure you are saving enough from your income; and (2) set your annual savings goal. If you haven't accomplished both, you're not ready to concentrate on investing. The groundwork just hasn't been done. On the first point, you can't invest properly if you don't have the money put aside to invest with. On the second, you have to know where you're going and if you've come far enough along each year.

So let's say you're ready for the next step. Perhaps you are already an investor. Maybe you even own some stocks and mutual funds. But if you're like most people, you haven't established any sense of order in your investing. Without a doubt, the temptation to invest randomly is greater than ever. There are more influences than ever trying to get you to buy stocks, bonds, mutual funds, and dozens of other kinds of investments. Tips and rumors of hot stocks are rampant as TV and newspapers wade deeper and deeper into investment reporting. Many people, enticed by articles and ads touting the latest hot mutual fund, wind up after a few years with perhaps a dozen funds with no coordination among them.

If you fall into this class of fund consumer, chances are you have a huge problem of redundancy among your funds. Sure, some of them are so-called large-cap funds that buy only huge corporations, while some may be small-cap funds that stay with up-and-comers. But there is more to diversification among funds than that. For instance, do you know which of your stock funds are growth funds and which are value funds? Which are equity-income? Got any midcaps? And how about the balance of industries among your stock funds? Many fund managers are enamored of technology stocks, for instance. If all or most of your stock funds have big commitments to technology, the next time that sector takes a dive, most of your wonderfully diversified funds will plunge, too.

Then there's the question of growth versus income. The 1980s saw a long bull market in bonds—so long that many younger investors weren't aware that there was ever much downside in bond investing. Then came the bust of the 1990s, and one of investing's cyclical lessons was learned again. What was so sad for many investors, in fact, was that they were probably too young to be in bond funds in the first place. Growth should be the primary, maybe even the sole, emphasis of any investor who is more than a few years away from retirement. For those who expect to retire early, young, and rich, growth is just about the only way to go. But you have to do it in a reasoned, orderly way. And that's the first lesson in this lesson-heavy chapter on investing.

It's Asset Allocation, Stupid

And it's really simple. Just make sure you select a portfolio with the right mix of stocks and bonds, and make careful adjustments every 10 years or so. That's it. And here is why this rule is so overarchingly important: Most of your profit from investing comes directly from getting the right combination of assets. A seminal 1991 study by money managers Gary P. Brinson and Brian D. Singer and consultant Gilbert Beebower found that about 92% of investor returns comes from asset allocation. The other 8%, astonishingly, comes from picking the right stock, bond or fund and from the correct timing of your buying and selling.

Basic Rules for All Ages

As you'll see, you should shift your asset allocations as you get older. But some aspects of your investing ought to stay solid and unchanging, like beacons. There are five:

1. Make stocks your number one investment. As you move through this chapter and see how we recommend you allocate your money to different investments, one thing may startle you: Stocks dominate the mix. Let's make clear right now how important this insight is. Since 1926, stocks on average have whipped the competition by a huge margin: stocks have on average returned 10.3% a year before taxes, compared with 5% for long-term Treasury bonds and only 3.1% for cash investments like short-term Treasury bills. That last performance is just in line with inflation, which means that cash didn't really return anything over nearly 70 years. Yet poll after poll shows that the average U.S. household invests only about a quarter of its assets in stocks, half the amount it puts into fixed-income assets like bonds.

That means that just on the basis of general choice, the average American family is gaining only half as much as it should with its investments. And if asset allocation is not being done correctly—and you have to assume that in most homes it isn't—Americans by and large are getting only a fraction of the bang out of their investment dollar that they should be. That's a formula for retiring old and insecure. And it's sad, because it is totally unnecessary.

2. Invest through mutual funds. To follow our asset-allocation guidelines with stocks and bonds requires the time, talent, and knowledge of markets that few individual investors possess. The fact of the matter is that few investors are interested enough in the stock market alone to make the needed investment of time. So don't kid yourself, or be persuaded by some posturing stock jockey, that you can do it all yourself. Besides, some categories of investment—particularly international stocks and bonds and, to a lesser extent, small stocks and bonds in general—are best approached via mutual funds. For instance, it is difficult to follow most foreign stocks easily; and the high volatility of small stocks calls for constant monitoring. Instead, go for the diversification and professional management of mutual funds. (For more on buying individual funds, see Chapter 7: "How to Choose Mutual Funds.")

3. Stay the course. As we've already said, the overexposure in the media and generalized hype associated with mutual fund investing is one of the underappreciated reasons why many investors fail to make steady, sizable progress in their returns. The fund of the moment looks tantalizing, and the fund you already own sometimes looks bedraggled by comparison.

So why not switch out of your fund and into the winner? Because today's hero will be tomorrow's nobody. Count on it. Several recent studies indicate that people who buy load funds (those with a sales commission that can range to 5% or more) made as much as 20% more over the past 10 years than those who bought no-load funds. This would seem impossible unless managers of load funds are inherently more talented stock pickers than managers of no-load funds.

The real reason for the gap in performance: The load fund customers stayed with their funds largely because they had paid a stiff entry fee and didn't want to just throw it away. The no-load customers, on the other hand, felt freer to dump their fund as market conditions changed and other funds looked more enticing. So if you've chosen your funds well, there is rarely a reason to sell. Since most investors sell when an investment is down, selling usually means losing. Take to heart this sobering observation from Benjamin Graham, one of the guiding geniuses of stock investing: "The investor's chief problem—and even his worst enemy—is himself."

4. Put everything you can into your 401(k). Or your Individual Retirement Account (IRA), Keogh, 403(b), or other tax-deferred retirement plan. Because the money you put into one is usually not taxed, and particularly because that money is then allowed to compound untaxed until you take it out after retirement, these plans are by far the best place for your investments.

This example is dramatic evidence: Say you saved $5,000 a year for 30 years, got an 8% rate of return each year, and paid taxes at 28%. After the 30 years, your fund would be worth $288,585. But if instead you put that same $5,000 into a 401(k) plan at work each year and received the same 8% return, you would wind up with $611,729—more than double the amount earned outside the tax-deferred account. Since most employers who offer 401(k) plans also match your contribution with one of their own—say, 50 cents on the dollar—the typical account would grow even faster than the example shows.

Once you reach the point where you are putting as much as you can into your 401(k)—nearly $10,000 or 15% of your salary—and have more money to invest, consider opening an IRA. This is a particularly good idea for people in their twenties who may not have a 401(k) available at work. If your adjusted gross income (your total income minus a few tax-favored items like alimony) is $25,000 or less and you're single, or $40,000 or less and you're married and file jointly, you can deduct a full $2,000 IRA contribution each year.

If, on the other hand, you are not eligible for an IRA deduction, you might still consider opening an IRA if you have no 401(k) at work. The tax-free compounding alone would be worth it. And you can make the saving process painless by having your IRA contribution deducted from your checking or savings account each month by the mutual fund, broker, or bank where you have set up your account.

5. Allocate *all* of your investments. A common error people make is forgetting one or more portions of their entire portfolio of investments when figuring out asset allocation. Let's say, for instance, that you are concentrating your saving or investing on a company 401(k). But you may also have a separate account holding company stock that you have been accumulating. Or you have a fund, an annuity, or maybe even a stash of U.S. savings bonds. Include every last one of these investments when you compute your asset allocation, or else your portfolio will be out of balance.

Now for the nitty-gritty. Following are four model portfolios of investments that will yield a well-balanced asset-allocation mix—for your twenties to thirties, thirties to forties, forties to fifties, and fifties to sixties.

PORTFOLIO 1: 20s TO EARLY 30s

Asset mix:
10% large-company stocks
25% midcap stocks
15% small-company stocks
30% international stocks
15% intermediate-term corporate bonds
 5% convertible or high-yield bonds

As you can see from the above table, we are recommending that the youngest investors should put no less than 80% of their money into stock funds. Since in this phase you are farthest away from needing retirement money to live on, it makes perfect sense to put a maximum amount into the kind of investment that pays best over time.

Remember that when you are diversified and your investments are being carefully shepherded by professional mutual fund managers, you may face some frightening short-term losses along the way, but in the long run you will do best with stocks. So let's take this advice a step further: If you can make it through the occasional stock market storms

without losing sleep, by all means increase your stock allocation to 100% while you are young. You have nothing to
lose but a few more years of your working life. You have
nothing to gain but an earlier retirement.

If you are a true novice at investing, and you have only
$1,000 or so to start you off, your best bet is to buy just
one fund that holds large-company stocks and has a good
long-term performance record under the same manager.
(Again, more on buying a fund in Chapter 7.) If stocks
make you nervous, be aware that this type of fund collects
blue chips that don't have the stomach-churning volatility
of smaller, less-tested stocks. But let's say you want to get
your feet wet with a stock fund that's even tamer than that.
In such a case, seek out a balanced or asset-allocation fund.
Both these categories of fund split their holdings between
stocks and bonds; the bonds are like ballast shielding the
overall portfolio from the risk even a blue-chip stock fund
faces. But as you gain experience as a stock investor, and
as you see that what goes down comes up again and you
make real headway, chances are you will become less risk-
averse. When that happens, move back into the pure-stock
funds, where the ride, though bumpier, is far more rewarding.

When your stash grows to the $10,000 level, it's time to
branch out into midcaps (stocks of companies with annual
revenues from $1 billion to $5 billion) and small-caps (those
with revenues of $1 billion or less). With 25% in midcaps,
15% in small-caps, 30% in international funds, and only
10% in the more stable large-cap funds, you can see what
is happening. You are not simply diversifying; you are ex-
tending your risk. The reason is that the highest returns in
the coming years are widely expected to come in smaller
stocks and those of other nations. Historically, in fact, small

stocks have outpaced larger ones, with average annual returns of 12.4% versus 10.3% for blue chips.

International stocks have soared and ebbed in recent
years, making them considerably more volatile than domestic shares. When you begin buying international funds,
then, consider again your stomach for churning markets,
because you have to expect a high level of volatility on this
front for the foreseeable future. Currency swings alone can
be a huge factor that you don't have to face if you keep to
domestic stock funds. But as the global economy asserts
itself, experts predict that there will be nowhere to hide
from the presence of world stocks—not, at least, if you
are out to achieve big returns over the coming years. One
recommendation: As you start out, stay away from so-
called emerging market funds—those that specialize in such
developing economies as Latin America and the smaller
countries of the Far East. However, since the stocks of those
countries are widely expected to offer the most sensational
growth opportunities of the next few decades, remember
that as you get more used to market dips and as your nest
egg grows, you may well want to add one or more such
funds to your mix later on.

One more complication on the stock front for now: Get to
know which of your funds are value and which are growth
funds. As you get older, you will probably want to have
both types in your portfolio because each brings a particular
strength. Value funds buy out-of-favor stocks with prices
that do not fully reflect their real value. Growth stock funds
go for stocks with fast-growing earnings, even if they feature premium prices. But no one knows when the stock
market will be responding to value and when it will be
geared to growth.

One sensible recommendation: Try to keep about 60%
of your stock allocation in value funds and the rest in growth

funds. When newspapers and magazines report on mutual fund performance, they often indicate which style each stock fund follows.

Now a word about your fixed-income allocation. As the table indicates, put 15% of your money in investment-grade bonds, those with intermediate maturities of five to 10 years. This segment of the mix is the most solid and least volatile of all. In fact, studies have shown that intermediates yield returns virtually as good as those of 30-year bonds, with only half the volatility.

Think of this portion as the ballast of your portfolio. Things get a bit racy with the rest of the fixed-income allocation, as you put 5% of your money into either a convertible bond fund or a high-yield bond fund. The first offers a good chance at capital gains when bonds the fund owns are "converted" into common stock. The second increases your risk via portfolios of "junk" bonds; diversification and careful picking can increase your yields to more than 9% without the danger of buying individual junk bonds.

A special note on buying bond funds: Because bonds can't reach for the kind of performance over time that stocks enjoy, buy only those bond funds with annual fees below 1%; many fine ones nick you very gently, at less than .5%. And stick with no-load funds in this category. You can find all the relevant information on fees and charges in each fund's prospectus or in fund listings in major newspapers and magazines.

Bottom line: Over several years, you can figure out how well your portfolio will perform during this initial phase of your investment life. Based on past returns, our configuration of 80% stocks and 20% bonds is likely to increase by an annual average of 9%. Possible expected return can run as high as 25% and as low as 7% in any one year.

PORTFOLIO 2: EARLY 30s TO 40s

Asset mix:
10% large-company stocks
25% midcap stocks
10% small-cap stocks
25% international stocks
20% intermediate corporate bonds
10% international bonds

If you go by the book, now is the time to reduce risk somewhat, especially if you have taken on the responsibility of a family and a mortgage. Our table suggests that you drop from 80% in stocks to 70%, heavying up on more stable bonds. In addition, by trimming your small-stock exposure from 15% to 10% and international stocks from 30% to 25%, you further tame down your mix.

This is as far as most people in this age group should go in recognizing the need for financial stability. After all, you still have two decades or so before normal retirement. In fact, those with more daring and less family responsibility might even want to stay closer to the 80% stock guideline laid down for the youngest group.

If you follow the allocation to the letter, you will be switching the money you have just trimmed from stocks into your intermediate-term bond fund, which would grow from 15% to 20% of the portfolio.

On the fixed-income side, you'll notice that an international bond fund has been added as 10% of the portfolio as a diversification note, standing in for the more daring high-yield or convertible fund. The international exposure in bonds is strongly diversifying because fixed-income markets in the United States and abroad tend to move in different directions. The risk here is of the foreign exchange variety. Even disinterested Americans have gotten used to headlines in the TV evening news and in the morning papers about the dollar sinking against the Japanese yen or the German mark. But again, if your money rides the wavy foreign exchange markets for a good decade or so, you should more than make up for the occasional dip and dive.

Bottom line: You should look for average annual returns of about 8.75%, with a risk of losing up to 5.75% and a chance of gaining as much as 23.25% in any single year.

PORTFOLIO 3: EARLY 40s TO 50s

Asset mix:
20% large-company stocks
20% midcap stocks
10% small-company stocks
20% international stocks
25% intermediate Treasuries/munis
 5% international bonds

While your overall split remains at 70% stocks, 30% bonds, some small rejiggering leaves you somewhat safer. This is as it should be: you are getting older and closer to retirement, and you are likely experiencing the tightest family budget period, thanks to college bills. Lowering your risk soothes your nerves and guards your winnings so far. But you still have plenty of growth in your mix because your added safety is accomplished primarily by doubling the proportion of large-cap blue chips to 20% from 10% and dropping both midcaps and international stocks from 25% to 20%.

Another way to increase the stability of your portfolio is by tilting the stock portion away from growth funds and toward both value funds and equity-income funds. By going for low-priced stocks, value funds normally don't fall as far as growth funds do when the stock market takes a tumble. The same is true of equity-income funds, which fall less than growth funds largely because they tend to buy more stable dividend-paying stocks. There's a price to be paid for all this peaceableness, of course: When the bull market is roaring ahead, value and equity-income entrants don't rise as fast or as high as pure growth stocks.

On the bond front, you can lock in the ultimate in safety by moving completely out of corporates and cutting the internationals in half and putting the proceeds—fully a quarter of your entire portfolio—into Treasury notes. These are U.S. Treasury issues ranging in maturity from one to 10 years. Depending on the direction of the bond market at any given time, Treasury notes yield nearly as much as 30-year Treasury bonds without the long-term commitment and consequent higher volatility. And usually it is a better idea to forgo the management fees associated with Treasury bond funds and go directly for the notes themselves. (You can buy them through a brokerage house or save even that fee and go directly to the seller, the Federal Reserve. For information, call 202-452-3000 or your local Federal Reserve branch.)

An alternative to Treasury notes would be a municipal bond fund for investors in the 28% federal tax bracket (or above). Again, look for muni funds with annual fees that are well under 1% and that hold bonds rated A or better.

Bottom line: Heavying up on large-cap stocks will hold your probable risk of loss to 5% and permit a possible gain of as much as 21% in any year. Average returns: 8%.

PORTFOLIO 4: EARLY 50s TO 60s

Asset mix:
20% large-cap stocks
15% midcap stocks
 5% small-company stocks
20% international stocks
40% muni bonds or T-notes

If you were lucky enough to consult, say, your grandparents at this point in your life, you might receive priceless pieces of wisdom about the art of aging gracefully. But when they got to finances, you would probably receive truly bum advice—heartfelt, but nonetheless bad. They would no doubt tell you that now is the time to convert all of your assets into bank certificates of deposit or, at most, supersafe bonds like those issued by the U.S. Treasury. You could forgive them for being wrong, because when they retired they could reasonably look forward to a fairly limited number of golden years. But since you are looking at 30 or more of those years, getting rid of your growth investments would almost certainly ensure that you run out of money long before you die, unless you are a multimillionaire. And for anyone contemplating really early retirement—before 55 or so—such a move would be a long-term disaster, considering that any fixed-income investment or pension would be worth just half as much in 15 years if inflation runs at only a modest 4% annually.

So you'll still need growth and lots of it. That's why our asset-allocation model, while dropping from 70% in stocks, will still maintain a 60–40 balance between stocks and fixed-income instruments. Large-cap stocks hold at 20%, as do internationals, but midcaps drop from 20% to 15%, and small-cap exposure is cut in half from 10% to 5%.

As a further bow to safety, the entire 40% income allocation is swept into U.S. Treasury notes or municipal bonds.

Bottom line: Our model portfolio shoots for average annual returns of 7.5%, with risk of loss averaging 4.5% and possible gain ranging as high as 19.5% in any year.

Now that you know how much of which kinds of funds you should own at each stage in your life, the next step is selecting the right specific funds. We turn to that question in the next chapter.

CHAPTER 7

How to Choose Mutual Funds

It's often said that investments aren't bought, they're sold. If you've ever been on the receiving end of a "cold call" from a hungry young stockbroker, you know the story. Salesmen or ads or hyped newspaper articles can steamroll you into buying more out of excited ignorance than dispassionate knowledge. And that insight applies as much to mutual funds as to any stock, bond, or other investment.

Today there are over 7,000 mutual funds you can buy—more than the total number of stocks traded on the New York Stock Exchange and the American Stock Exchange combined. Brokers use this profusion and resulting confusion as a lever. Their argument: There are just too many funds for the individual to decide what to buy. Then—surprise!—you wind up being sold funds marketed by the very brokerage house that employs the broker who is selling you the funds. Some choice. Or you read the breathless stories that appear in newspapers and magazines four times a year, describing the latest "hot" funds, then you run out and buy them. But next year they're not hot anymore, and you go through the same cycle, jettisoning last year's heroes and grabbing on to this year's.

That's no way to be an investor. In the long run you wind up either losing money or at least not making as much as you should. And, of course, you miss out on the opportunity to retire young and rich. The aim of this chapter is to teach you enough about mutual funds so that you can either buy them yourself or at least be able to monitor buying and selling by your financial adviser. (See Chapter 9 for advice on choosing an adviser.)

The Ideal: To Buy and to Hold

Unless you are a close student of mutual fund activity who spends hours every week checking out market shifts, comings and goings of fund managers, and other vital fund news, join the majority of mutual fund investors: those who sincerely want their money to grow but lack the interest and time to manage that growth. Isn't that what you're paying the fund managers to do anyway? If that fairly describes you, common sense tells you that you had better buy your funds with care, because you will be leaving them in the hands of their managers for long stretches of time, during which you will be proccupied with many other facets of your life.

Buy and hold, in fact, has long been honored by some of the most astute students of the stock market. And if it's a viable approach to stock investing, it should be even more so when it comes to stock funds. A stock, for instance, can fall prey to any number of problems that demand you sell it. But a well-managed fund that is part of a well-run fund family, even if it never leads the list of performers in any one year, ought to bring excellent returns over time.

Unfortunately the situation is considerably stickier when it comes to bond funds. One of the safest investment moves you can make is to buy a high-quality bond, hold it to maturity, receive your interest along the way, and get your principal back at the end. There's no interest rate risk because the rate is set and predictable when you buy. And there's no market risk because you are willing to wait out the term of the bond and not try to sell in the hurly-burly of the bond market, which is subject to unpredictable interest rate fluctuations. But when you get into a bond fund, whose managers buy and sell bonds all the time, you are subject to market risk *and* interest rate risk. So it's at least as essential that you place your money with bonds funds whose managers have demonstrated their ability to come out ahead over time.

The rest of this chapter relates the most important points to look for and the major pitfalls to avoid when buying a fund. It ends with a short and to-the-point discussion of when you should give up and sell a fund.

Loads, No-Loads, and Fees

How much should you pay a mutual fund for its services? Back in the bullish 1980s, many investors refused to take this issue seriously. Why worry about a few percentage points, they reasoned, when you're making an easy 15%, 20%, or more each year in the market? But it's different today. Few stock market specialists believe that we'll see anything like those years again. That is why you should take a closer look at total return—your profit when everything is taken into account. That's not just gains in the market and dividends from stock funds; not just gains in the market and interest in bond funds. It's all income added up and costs subtracted.

This leads us to the noisiest running feud in the entire world of mutual funds: Should you buy load funds or no-load funds? No-loads, for those just starting out, are mutual funds that you buy directly from the fund company without any load or sales charge. Load funds, by contrast, are those that are sold by stockbrokers or financial planners, who collect a sales charge typically around 4.5% but sometimes as high as 8.5%.

If you study history, you could go crazy trying to determine which has done better, loads or no-loads. If you're wise, you will come away with the conviction that the load factor has nothing at all to do with fund performance. A recent study by Morningstar Inc. and reported in the February 1995 issue of **Money** magazine came up with the eight most dependable funds in America—the eight stock funds that beat the three- and five-year increases of the benchmark Standard & Poor's 500 index and of the average equity fund. Four were loads, four were no-loads.

So what should you do now? It depends to a surprising extent on how disciplined an investor you are. That's because of two key factors, one favoring loads and the other favoring no-loads.

Buy load funds if you think you are apt to be so frightened by a market drop or so smitten by the next hot fund of the month that you'll keep shifting in and out of different funds. This, as we've said, is the surest way to lose money. What is so instructive is that recent studies indicate that people invested in load funds, because they have committed to hefty sales charges, tend to stay put longer than no-load investors, who are much more apt to flit about. That explains why so many people do so much better in load funds over time.

Buy no-load funds if you can maintain discipline while others panic. The reason is simple: If no-loads are just as good as loads, why pay the sales charge? Particularly these days, when profits won't be coming as fast and thick as they were in the 1980s, putting the equivalent of a sales charge to work as part of your investment can make a real difference.

Management fees can be an even greater expense than loads if you hold a fund for a number of years. So the argument about getting as much of your money into the investment itself and not losing it through expenses goes doubly here. In general, try to keep the annual management fee on your stock funds, particularly large-caps and mid-caps, below 1%. Among stock funds you can make an exception for small-stock funds and international funds, which are generally more expensive to run. But have a strong reason for going above 1.3% on a small-cap and 1.5% on diversified international stock funds. As for bond funds, the rule is even stricter: With few exceptions, avoid any with annual fees that exceed .9%. As you look around, in fact, you will find highly regarded stock and bond funds with fees under one-half or even one-quarter of 1%. Also try to stay clear of funds that feature **12b-1 fees,** which are annual charges that pay for a fund's marketing costs and can skim off an additional .15% to 1% of your money. Load funds are where you are apt to find 12b-1 fees: nearly nine out of 10 broker-sold funds carry them. But nearly three out of 10 no-loads also charge 12b-1s.

marries value and growth investing, and on and on. You get the idea.

The outcome of all this excitement is that too many small investors who don't read much beyond the headlines in the business pages of their newspapers wind up holding dozens of mutual funds. What's wrong with that? First of all, it becomes progressively more difficult to keep track of your funds. And if you've been buying hot ones, chances are they will cool off deeply in a year or two and lag the markets for the rest of your life if you hang on to them. Second, investors holding more than a handful of funds will almost surely find out that they have huge overlaps that may be dangerous. For instance, many otherwise diversified funds hold huge wads of technology stock in their portfolios. Some major funds have up to 25% of their holdings in technology stocks, two and a half times the weighting of such issues in the Standard & Poor's 500 stock index.

This not only reduces diversification, a bedrock virtue of investing in mutual funds in the first place; it also means that when one fund manager decides it's time to dump technology issues, his move might cause a stampede that could hurt all those funds with big commitments to these stocks. If you're left holding only one such fund, the damage is a lot less than if you have, say, half a dozen growth funds overweighted in tech stocks.

Experts advise that few investors should hold more than a dozen funds. Beginners with only a few thousand dollars to invest hardly need more than one or two. And if you follow our asset-allocation suggestions in Chapter 6, you need not invest in more than half a dozen funds.

It's also wise to limit your purchases to a couple of fund families. These are companies—such as Fidelity, T. Rowe Price, Vanguard, and Twentieth Century—that offer a wide selection of stock, bond, and money funds. Administration and paperwork is kept to a minimum this way, and expenses can also be kept down if you do any switching among funds within the same families. Some fund families—notably Fidelity and Charles Schwab—have branched out into networks that offer hundreds of funds from dozens of different families under the same roof.

Four Added Points to Consider

As a long-term fund investor, you'll be happier, less nervous, and better off all around if you shrewdly choose every fund you buy. You already know you will be in the market for one or more large-cap, midcap, small-cap, and international stock funds, plus three or four kinds of bond funds. You've been clued in on loads versus no-loads and the elements of risk. Here are four additional judgments that will help you zero in on the choicest picks:

1. Don't overlook index funds. These are the funds that buy all the stocks in a given index, such as the Standard & Poor's 500, and thereby mimic the performance of those stocks as a whole. Today you can buy a range of index funds for large stocks like the S&P 500, for small stocks (the Wilshire or Russell indexes), for international securities, and so on. Champions of index funds like their steady if unspectacular performance, their usually low fees, and their tendency to cost you less in taxes because of their low turnover. As your investment stake grows and you get older, you may want to turn to one or more index funds for your stock or bond asset allocations. If you do, you might consider putting your taxable money in index funds and keeping your tax-deferred 401(k)s and IRAs in actively managed funds.

2. Do pass on sector funds. Some of the larger fund families offer sector funds, which invest exclusively in the stocks of a single industry (like health care or technology) or commodity (like gold). These are among the most volatile funds of all, often landing at the top of the performance charts one year and at the bottom the next. They won't give you the steady advances that well-diversified funds will.

3. Ditto smart-aleck funds. These are the ones that practice market timing, moving massively into or out of stocks according to their readings of technical indicators. No one has been able successfully to time the market, over long periods, and market timers are a colorful example of winner-loser streaks, with emphasis on loser. That's why you'll see feature stories in the press about the brave financial analyst who single-handedly called the latest market swing. Chances are you'll either hear no more of that momentary star or read a year or two later that he or she has just made a disastrously wrong market call this time.

Another variety of smart-aleck fund is the type that bets a significant proportion of its entire portfolio on a single stock. This approach to stock picking is for people with a richer taste for risk than the average investor should entertain. So if you see a fund putting 8% or more of its money on one stock, back away.

4. Stay with the track stars. As we said before, the fund stars of the moment tend to be momentary flashes. The real winners are those with the solidest long-term records. Don't consider a fund that lags over at least the past three years.

How to Get All That Info

We've laid out a healthy diet of data for you to collect— about loads and management fees, the families the funds belong to, types of funds, turnover, long-term performance records, and more. Let's stop here and say this: It's not a hard job, and you don't have to be an investing nerd to absorb it. Here's how to go about it.

First off, if you are buying load funds through a broker or financial planner, or no-load funds recommended by a financial planner, *get that pro to do the spadework for you*. This is a particularly fair demand when you are dealing with a broker or planner who is about to get a fat commission for selling you the fund. This is part of his or her job, so don't do business with anyone who balks at full disclosure. (For more on choosing and dealing with a professional adviser, see Chapter 9.)

If you are doing the research yourself, you will find most of what you need in the prospectus that the fund family sends to you with your application forms. You would do well also to consult the latest quarterly peformance reports that appear in major newspapers and personal finance magazines. Your local public library probably carries the magazines and may even subscribe to mutual fund–advisory newsletters. Who knows? You might even find it all fascinating.

When to Sell

This section was nearly omitted for one very good reason: If you choose carefully, you will likely be able to hang on to your funds for the long run. That being said, there are two generally valid reasons for selling a mutual fund:

1. Performance has been inexcusably poor. There are many times in the life of a fund when it suffers a sinking spell. When this happens, you can't just overlook it—if it doesn't snap back, your long-term retirement plans may be in trouble. On the other hand, there may be a very good and excusable reason for the drop, such as when an entire group (like small-cap stocks) or an approach (like value investing) falls into market disfavor. So if a fund you own has a one-year loss or just stagnates for a couple of years, check it out. You may find that the second reason for dumping a fund is the operative one here.

2. There has been a change in management. Like a restaurant with a new chef, a mutual fund with a new manager can become a wholly different entity, serving up lackluster results. It is wise to check with your fund every six months or at least once a year to see if there's been a change of manager. If there has, call the fund family and ask straight out if the new manager plans to continue the same investing strategy. If not, and you are not happy with what you hear, it may be a signal to sell. Even if you get a pledge that the approach will not change, keep checking performance to make sure the new person can actually carry out the fund's philosophy as successfully as the star he or she has replaced.

CHAPTER 8

Getting the Most out of Savings Plans

It's time to talk seriously about the retirement savings plan that your employer offers you: your 401(k) if you're employed by a for-profit company; your 403(b) if you work for a tax-exempt organization; or even your Keogh or SEP plan if you are self-employed. Here is the central issue about these plans, and you should take a moment to let it sink in:

These are without question your number one most powerful and important retirement savings vehicles. Yet they are badly abused and mismanaged by most people who have them. This chapter is about running your plan so it produces results equal to its capacity.

We'll explain. If you want to retire young and rich, or even at 65 with enough to live comfortably for the rest of your life, you will need a nest egg that draws from three sources. First is Social Security, but as we've seen, that will probably be the smallest part. Then there are the savings and investments you make on your own, outside your corporate savings plan. This portion will probably fall somewhere in between in size, and to be realistic, for most people it will be tiny or even nonexistent; most Americans just don't save that well. The third portion of your stash, the 401(k) or other tax-deferred plan, will in all likelihood be the biggest piece of your pie. (Your employer may also give you a traditional pension, but many don't, and even so, that doesn't involve any saving by you.)

It's important to understand the tremendous investment energy that one of these plans unleashes. Since you are most likely to have a 401(k), we'll use that as our example, although our argument covers all the plans in general. When you tell your payroll department how much to siphon from your paychecks each year into your 401(k)—the maximum allowable in 1995 is $9,240—100% of that money goes to work for you because it is untaxed.

Then many employers match your contribution at rates of 50 cents or more on the dollar. In addition, any profits— dividends, interest, and capital gains—are also untaxed until you start withdrawing money after age 59½. Finally, all these dollars compound at such increasingly furious rates that in the long run more of the money in your account comes from compound interest than from the money you have been putting in. It's a bravura peformance that you could never get out of investments made outside such a protected plan.

So it's only good sense that you closely watch that 401(k) and make decisions that will help it grow to the max. But if you're like most of the 401(k) holders polled in study after study, you are making a powerful thoroughbred trot around the track when he could be winning races. People tend to put their money into the safest options, the ones that deliver safe but modest income year after year. Instead they should be letting most of their dough ride on growth options, which admittedly can suffer bruising short-term losses but always come back to win big over the long term.

According to Ibbotson Associates, a highly respected financial research and consulting firm in Chicago, here are the compound average annual rates of return over 60 years ending in 1993:

Large stocks (S&P 500)	11.4%
Small stocks	15.1%
Long-term corporate bonds	5.5%
Long-term government bonds	5.1%
30-day Treasury bills	3.9%

Keeping these rates of return in mind, let's see what the difference would be over time between the conservative and the growth stash. Say you managed to put $500 a month into your tax-deferred account for 30 years. Here is what you would wind up with in your 401(k) or 403(b) or Keogh at the end:

At a 4% rate, roughly the return from keeping all your money in supersafe Treasury bills: **$458,000.**

At a 12% rate, roughly the return from keeping all your money in large-cap stocks: **$3,248,000.**

There, in a nutshell, is the path to take when your goal is to retire young and rich.

What's really so wasteful about the way people mismanage their 401(k)s is that in recent years the number of options available to them have opened up dramatically, prodded by federal regulations creating incentives for companies to increase their choices. The result is that most companies with 401(k)s offer no fewer than four funds to choose from, and many offer 10 or more. The most common choices offered, beginning with the least risky, are government bond funds; guaranteed investment contracts (GICs), which are fixed-income instruments generally paying somewhat more than government bonds; balanced funds; equity-income funds; growth funds; and the employer's own stock. Many companies are also adding international funds, small-company funds, and asset-allocation funds.

Again, however—almost as if there were a curse on investment self-management—studies have shown that when the options grow too numerous, many employees get so confused, they throw up their hands and drop out of the plans entirely. This is sad and unnecessary, because the care and feeding of a 401(k) is really quite simple if you follow a few guidelines.

• **Contribute as much as you can.** Here is the way to invest: First, max out on your 401(k). If you have tried but failed to do so, it's time to go over your budget and cut back, because this is the absolute foundation of your retirement dream. You must be putting the most you can in the plan or all bets are off; you're just not being serious. Second, when you are able to put the full amount into your 401(k), then begin building a portfolio of investments outside the plan.

• **Try never to take anything out of your plan.** Many companies allow employees to borrow from their 401(k)s under favorable conditions. Resist this blandishment. The whole idea of a special tax-deferred account is compromised if the money in it is not compounding maximally at all times. Many people are tempted to take the money and spend it down when they change employers. They of course incur the 10% federal penalty for early withdrawals made before age 59½, plus regular income tax. This double bite can consume nearly half of the return built up by the investments inside the 401(k). Instead, if you transfer the proceeds from your old employer's plan to your new employer's, they can go on growing without any interruption or depletion.

• **Practice asset allocation and stick with it.** The apportionment of your money among mutual funds, following the asset-allocation models laid out in Chapter 6, should be no different when it comes to your 401(k). For example, when you are in your twenties, stash 80% of your money in stock funds, putting 10% into large-cap funds, 25% in midcaps, 30% into international funds, and 15% into small-caps. Then put the other 20% into bond funds, with 15% going to corporates and 5% to a convertible or high-yield bond fund. In the same way, follow the models for your thirties, forties, and fifties. You may find that you can't follow our allocation models exactly inside your 401(k). For example, say your employer's plan does not offer any international fund. In that case, the 30% you would have devoted to an international fund can be spread evenly among the other stock fund choices.

Then, when you begin to build your independent portfolio outside your 401(k), you might start out buying an international fund and, as that grows, rejigger the allocations inside your 401(k) to take the international fund into account. In other words, your allocation should be based on all your investments together, not just your 401(k) on the one hand or your other portfolio on the other. And remember that the virtues of asset allocation are compromised if you don't follow the models closely.

• **Be sensible about your company's stock.** Many employers make their stock so attractive to employees, some 401(k) accounts become dangerously underdiversified with an overabundance of company stock. One come-on is increasing the amount the company will put up in matching employee contributions—for example, throwing in a dollar for each employee dollar for the purchase of company stock versus only 50 cents on the dollar for buying other investments. Some companies even launched their 401(k)s offering only their own stock to put into the plan. The idea, of course, was to help support the market price of the stock. But a healthy diversification was one reason federal rules strongly encourage a real choice of five or more funds in a 401(k).

So how much of your company's stock should you be holding? That depends on how good a stock you honestly believe it to be. Company employees are in an enviable position to judge the health of its stock. So first of all, you might figure out where your company's stock would go if you were to put it into one of the stock funds in your 401(k). Would it be in the growth fund portfolio? Or is it more a blue chip belonging in equity-income? Whatever it is, figure your company stock as part of that fund. So if you are supposed to have, say, 20% of your money in a large-cap fund and your 401(k) features an equity-income fund full of large-caps, and you feel safe having 10% of your money invested in your company's stock, cut back your equity-income fund to 10% of the total too, so you still wind up with 20% in large-caps.

• **Refigure your portfolio no more than twice a year.** One of the most dangerous temptations for some employees is to call the 800 number of the institution that maintains the funds for your company's 401(k) and obsessively move your money around. Many plans permit participants to do this on a daily basis, and apparently the feeling of power it imparts can be intoxicating.

Here's a common scenario: The stock market moves dramatically. It doesn't matter in which direction, because we are not talking about rational behavior. If it moves down, excited investors will want to take advantage of the drop to switch their investments to riskier, more aggressive choices. This is actually a smart impulse in general, but it has to be harnessed to a disciplined plan of investing like asset allocation. Otherwise it is merely a hysterical flailing about. If stocks prices accelerate upward, many investors are consumed by an irresistible desire to get aboard while the getting is good. This is generally a destructive impulse and is the basis for what market experts describe as the speculative froth that characterizes a "toppy" market—that is, one that has risen to its peak and is poised for a collapse.

The one real value of being able to move money around inside your 401(k) is to keep your asset allocation on target. For instance, you may need to move some money out of a fund that has been surging and into one that has been slumping in order to regain the prescribed mix. Also, as you move from one decade to the next, you will need to reallocate according to the plan.

One final note about moving around your 401(k) money. In the coming years, it is likely that your employer will continue adding choices to the funds in your plan. As we said, currently the average number of options is five, with many companies offering 10 or more. As far as we could find out, the biggest choice at present is 41 separate funds. As your options expand, you should start comparing the choices within each asset class. For instance, say your company offers two large-company growth funds. It will be important for you to check out the performance record of both funds to make sure you are in the better of the two. If, however, you find that their styles and portfolios are different while their track records are both exemplary, you may want to split your money between the two. By exercising simple common sense and avoiding the extremes of shifting around (too much and too little), you will easily become a first-rate manager of your 401(k).

CHAPTER 9

Getting the Right Kind of Help

It's an immense job, no doubt about it. You are expecting to accumulate a stash perhaps well in excess of a million dollars while at the same time establishing a graceful home, educating your kids, taking exciting vacations, and availing yourself of dozens of smaller goods and services that tug at your budget in a consumer society. Maybe the wisest expenditure you could make would be to pay someone to advise you, even guide you to your goal. Maybe, just maybe, you aren't in a position to make it all the way on your own.

There are several kinds of advisers you can turn to—primarily financial planners, money managers, stockbrokers, and insurance company salespeople. The trouble is that if you link up with the wrong one, you could be wandering into a nightmare far worse than anything you could concoct on your own. Archives of the Securities and Exchange Commission and the National Association of Securi-

81

ties Commissioners are awash in stories relating how some financial planner or broker or insurance salesman put unwitting clients into devastatingly inappropriate investments in order to collect a high commission. Other horror tales, less sinister but still inexcusable, relate the stupidity and/or inexperience of otherwise well-meaning advisers.

This chapter will tell you what these pros can do for you and to you, and how to find the best and then use them to *your* best advantage.

Food for thought: As you read through this chapter, try to compare the value of paying for a pro's service with that of managing for yourself. There are two kinds of people in personal finance terms—those who can do it all alone and those who really need help.

Money magazine ran a lively article in its December 1994 issue called "The Best Personal Finance Managers in America." The piece consisted of profiles of a single, married couples with and without kids, retirees, and a single parent—all of whom had been doing a splendid job of handling their own finances—from astute investing to careful spending to sheltering capital gains from taxes to shopping for the best mortgage. **Money** magazine's editors and a panel of independent judges named 103 finalists out of 2,304 applicants entering a contest to find really successful do-it-yourself personal finance whizzes. The point here is simple: If you can go it alone, by all means do so. No hired hand will bring the care and insight to this job that you can bring yourself. But if you truly see that you don't have the interest or talent for the job, then find a pro—and soon.

Financial Planners

These are the generalists in the group. They are supposed to be trained to help you with your budgeting, investing, insurance, retirement planning, and so on. Because of this, financial planners have not been strong as investment money managers. In fact, many of them are so weak in their overall knowledge of personal finance that close observers of this burgeoning field believe incompetence to be a far greater problem than greed.

This introduction to the financial planner may sound grim, but don't be turned off. The hard part is finding a really good one. If you can, you will have a gem of great value. Here's how to go about it:

DRAW UP A LIST OF CANDIDATES. This is not as easy as it looks. You want quality here, not quantity, which means identifying at least three, preferably four or five, planners who come recommended by your lawyer, banker or accountant, or by friends or relatives who are satisfied clients of planners. Every candidate should have at least three years of experience in the field and sport the relevant certification: **certified financial planner (CFP)** is awarded by the International Board of Standards and Practices for Certified Financial Planners in Denver. Candidates have to pass a battery of tough exams on all of the areas of personal finance. **Chartered financial consultant (ChFC)** is awarded by the American College in Bryn Mawr, Pennsylvania, also based on rigorous exams, often to insurance agents or people with an insurance background.

You may run into two other terms when shopping for a planner. These designations are fine when the planner is also a CFP or ChFC; otherwise they suggest a pro who is highly focused only on investing or taxes. The **chartered**

financial analyst (CFA), awarded by the Association for Investment Management and Research in Charlottesville, Virginia, is often a money manager. The **personal financial specialist (PFS),** awarded by the American Institute of Certified Public Accountants in New York City, is often a CPA or other tax specialist.

INTERVIEW EACH CANDIDATE IN PERSON. This session should be free. If a planner insists on charging for it, cross him or her off your list and move on. If you feel rushed or you get the feeling that this person is not easy to talk to or get comfortable with, you needn't end the session abruptly; but you should also consider hiring such a planner only if he or she gets A-plus marks on every other score. Here are the questions to ask on that initial interview.

1. *How do you get paid?* The planner should quickly reveal to you which of three categories he or she falls into: fee-only, fee-and-commission, or commission-only planner. This is the basic division in the financial-planning profession, and no pro should be anything but totally honest and open about it. Then the planner should disclose exactly how he or she is compensated.

Fee-only planners are generally preferable because they receive no commissions for recommending financial products and so have no conflict of interest over those recommendations. You can buy an entire financial plan tailored to your needs for a fee of $2,000 to about $5,000. You can also pay a flat hourly fee, typically $100 or more per hour, for specific advice. The fee-only planner will usually recommend no-load mutual funds or life insurance. Some will actually manage portfolios of mutual funds for you, charging an annual fee of 1% or so of assets.

Fee-and-commission planners may receive flat fees of

$600 or so for a plan plus 3% to 5% commissions on investments that they sell to you. While your out-of-pocket expenses may seem lower than with a fee-only planner, you may in fact wind up paying two or three times more to the fee-and-commission planner when commissions are added in.

Commission-only planners operate under a total conflict-of-interest cloud, since they receive all of their income from the 3% to 5% commissions they charge for investments you buy from them.

2. *What kinds of financial planning do you do?* More and more planners specialize in retirement planning. But others focus on taxes, college costs, or small businesses. Make sure your planner's specialty matches your needs.

3. *Are you registered with the Securities and Exchange Commission and the securities department in your state?* This is considered by some experts as the absolute minimum qualification to look for. In short, if the planner hasn't registered with the SEC and is dealing with investment products, he or she may be violating federal law. Most states require that planners register with the state securities department. So while such registrations do not in any way guarantee competence or honesty, they do show that the planner is willing to comply with the law.

4. *Which financial products do you usually sell?* The answer to this one can be a solid-brass tip-off. As mentioned previously, only fee-and-commission planners and commission-only planners actually sell products. Fee-only planners sell services. So it is important to gauge how greedy planners who take commissions might get. For instance, if the planner sells primarily mutual funds, municipal bonds, govern-

ment securities, and the like, that's a good sign. But if he or she is quick to sell you a lot of life insurance, and follows that up with limited partnerships and unit trusts—all high-commission products—beware. One useful test: If a planner doesn't urge you to fully fund your employer's 401(k) and instead tries to sell you variable annuities, you can be sure he or she cares more about commissions than your welfare. Another test: Find out if the planner sells the mutual funds or insurance products of only his or her company. If so, you can be sure that there is no chance you will be offered the best choices.

5. *Have you ever been disciplined by any federal or state agency or professional body or been involved in arbitration with any clients?* No matter what the planner's answer is, you can verify it with the agency in question and back away if the record is bad.

6. *Will you give me a copy of your ADV Form, Part II?* This is the form the planner is supposed to file with the SEC and the state and to show prospective clients on request. It is a disclosure form that covers the planner's education, fees, business background, and investment style and whether he or she has ever been in trouble with a court or regulatory body. The SEC requires this form only from registered investment advisers, so planners who specialize in accounting or insurance needn't file an ADV. But anyone aiming to retire young and rich and looking for an adviser will necessarily want one who works with investments. So get that ADV, Part II. It is the single most revealing document about any investment-oriented planner—so much so that many planners will balk at giving you one. Don't take no for an answer.

7. *Will you give me the names of three people who have been your clients for at least two years?* Experienced planners who are confident about their work should be happy to comply. All they have to do is secure the permission of these clients for you to call them. When you do, simply ask them about their overall satisfaction with the planner's service, what level of returns they have been getting on their investments under the planner's guidance, and whether they plan to remain his or her clients. You might also ask if they know other clients and whether they too seem happy with the planner. You can even call these additional clients if you feel that any more probing is needed. In any case, never accept any excuse from a planner for not giving you some client names.

8. *Will you let me look at some of the plans you have developed for people like me?* You should be able to examine at least three full-scale plans to see if advice was geared to the needs of individual clients or whether it was mostly the same generalized boilerplate from one client to the other. Also ask for follow-up reports to find out how well the planner may have adjusted his or her advice to keep up with changes in the investment markets or in the client's situation.

DO A RECORD CHECK. After grilling your candidates and making a choice, there is one last chore you should do: Verify for yourself whether the planner has been the subject of any disciplinary actions. They are far from rare, so this exercise can be revealing and, of course, very important to you. First call the SEC (202-942-7040), then check with the securities department in your state (look under the state department of commerce in your local phone book). If the planner happens to be a member of the National Association of Securities Dealers (800-289-9999), find out if any actions have been taken by NASD against your prospective adviser. Some dirty tricks that turn up in these checks include churning accounts (too much buying and selling of investments to increase commissions) and having clients make out checks in his or her name instead of to the brokerage or fund family selling you the investment.

While all the questioning and checking may sound more like a grand jury probe than a search for a personal finance pro, you would feel otherwise if you could take a brief tour of the cases of fraud and incompetence that turn up each year. (For a rundown, see the section later in this chapter on brokers.) And remember that the right planner will likely be with you for many years to come, maybe even well into your retirement. He or she has to be worth the time, money, and trust you will be handing over year after year. Otherwise your planner could turn out to be your personal financial dream wrecker. Take no such chances with your future.

Money Managers

These are the pros whose services used to be reserved for the rich. But that is not the case anymore. You can have your own personal money manager with a stake of as little as $50,000 or so. Your money manager puts together a portfolio of stocks and bonds for you with the promise that it will beat the market over time. The idea has grown so popular with middle-class investors that so-called managed accounts are attracting more than $5 billion a year.

But is a money manager a good idea for you? Follow the judgment of trusted experts, and don't even consider going this route with a wad of less than $100,000. Otherwise transaction fees tend to be so expensive that you are better off with mutual funds.

Above $100,000, however, money managers have much to offer. Many of them actually deliver on their promise to earn higher-than-average returns. This, in fact, has been easier to do in recent years, when most mutual fund managers have tended to lag the averages. In addition, you enjoy much greater flexibility than with a mutual fund. For instance, you can ask your money managers to delay taking capital gains by selling winning stocks until next year instead of this year, deferring taxes on your profit. And while mutual funds are required under law to distribute a part of their capital gains each year, you can keep on racking up gains with stocks in your managed portfolio without paying any tax until the stock is sold. You can also express your own values or style, for example, by requesting that your money manager not buy tobacco stocks or that he or she buy aggressive growth stocks or shares in a sector of the economy to which you are particularly attracted.

If having a money manager appeals to you, then you should go through a process of selection similar to the one laid out in this chapter for financial planners. This time you needn't be quite so rigorous because money managers focus on only one area of finance—investing—and have to rise or fall on their performance there. (Judging a generalist, which most financial planners tend to be, is far less cut and dried.) Here's how to go about it.

Avoid 3% fees. This is a simple way to steer clear of brokerage wrap accounts, which are so expensive because of the fees that even a money manager who performs well would have trouble making you an above-average return. Typically, instead of the 1% or 2% a year that a money manager may charge, you get a prepackaged plan that wraps the money manager's services, brokerage fees, and other charges into a single 3% fee. Often you don't even get to talk to the money manager, but instead go through the broker or financial planner who sold you into the plan.

Go through a specialist unless you get a great referral. A few lucky people know someone—a friend or relative—who has used a money manager for years and has enjoyed high returns and genuine satisfaction. If you have such a contact, by all means use it. But if you don't, it's wise to get help from an independent specialist known as an **investment management consultant.** These are often stockbrokers who find money managers for clients. In return they receive the brokerage commissions that your money manager generates for your account.

Generally consultants refer you to small independent money managers who can give you individual attention. In addition, the brokers usually discount their commissions as much as 40% for money managers, so your total annual cost should not exceed 2% of the value of your portfolio. But many such money managers also charge 15% to 20% of the return they make on your money. For example, if you place $100,000 with a money manager who makes it grow to $125,000 in a year, you would pay him up to $5,000 in addition to commission costs. This may sound excessive, but many clients are happy to pay at this rate if their money manager pretty consistently whips the averages.

You can locate a talent scout in your area by calling the Institute for Investment Management Consultants (602-922-0090). This organization will recommend brokers with substantial work and educational experience. Any of these broker-consultants should have at least a dozen managers with different investing styles for you to choose from.

Monitor the records of at least three money managers. After the consultant makes recommendations, you have to make sure he or she is not simply handing you over to a money manager who shunts commissions his or her way. So check performance records back at least five years. Then check the manager's record with a benchmark that mirrors his or her style—like the Russell 2000 index for a manager who specializes in small-company stocks or the Russell earnings-growth index for a manager who buys growth stocks. The broker recommending the manager can provide you with such performance comparison data. You'll be able to tell if you have the stomach to hang on for the ups and downs experienced by a more aggressive manager or, conversely, whether a more conservative approach garners returns that are too tepid for your goals.

Make sure the manager is registered with the SEC. While this won't guarantee performance, it will mean that you can ask for the manager's ADV—the very revealing form we described to you above in the section on finding a financial planner. Remember, you get it all here—the manager's experience, style, fees, and record of any disciplinary actions taken against him or her by any regulatory agency.

Keep track of your pro's performance. You ought to be receiving from the broker who found your manager for you a quarterly breakdown of stocks and bonds in your portfolio, all buys and sells during the period, and a comparison of your holdings' performance with at least one index, like the S&P 500 or the Russell 2000.

The more aggressive the manager is, the more patient you need to be with fluctuations in returns. But just as there may be some heart-stopping downdrafts, there should also be lifts that outweigh the losses and sweep you ahead over time. So if your manager's returns lag not only the market but similar managers for a year or more, it's time to find out if his approach has changed or if he's not the stock picker he once was. Your consultant should be willing to discuss your concern and, if needed, find you a new manager.

Stockbrokers and Other Salespeople

If you ever consider using a stockbroker or a sales representative of an insurance or mutual fund company, chances are it is because one among these legions has called you on the phone and made a pitch. Our general advice to you is to give such cold calls the cold shoulder. In these instances, you don't end up buying something; it gets sold to you.

Such salespeople operate with an inherent conflict of interest. They are usually selling a product, whether it is a stock, bond, mutual fund, or insurance policy, that they are being told to promote. Either it is a product of the company they work for or it is a product being marketed by their company. As a result, there is not even a semblance of objectivity to the advice you will get from such professionals. They may call themselves financial planners, financial analysts, or investment bankers, but that ploy alone should tip you off that they are not leveling with you. They are salespeople first, last, and always.

So why tell you all this if the message is just "Don't"? Because the message is really "If." If a stockbroker passes a few simple tests you can put to him or her, just as you might put a planner or money manager through the paces, you may have found another one of those rare jewels who will actually help you make a lot of money. The run-of-the-cold-call broker today is not for you. But here are the characteristics of those who might be:

- Brokers whose recommendations are based on research they do on their own, not just on the often stale research handed out by their brokerage's securities analysts. The best brokers have always been independent stock pickers first and team players for their brokerages second.
- Brokers who actually own the stocks that are on their buy lists. This generally follows the point above about brokers doing their own research. This kind of self-confidence will surely boost yours in your broker.
- Brokers who won't bother you by trying to sell you the products of their brokerages, which are all too often heavily loaded with sales commissions and management fees. For instance, how can a broker justify asking a load of up to 8½% for recommending a mutual fund that—surprise!—is part of his employer's stable of funds?

    Aside from these points, your prospective broker should submit to some of the same questions we laid out for planners and money managers. In particular, make sure you get to talk to a few of his or her seasoned customers and get background information on education, experience, and investing style. Get fee and commission policies spelled out in black and white. And always call that toll-free hot line operated by the NASD (800-289-9999).

As a parting slap in the face on this subject, here are some numbers to think about whenever you contemplate hiring a financial-services pro of any kind to help you make money. The NASD regularly publishes statistics on the evildoers turned up by its hot line and other efforts to weed out unethical practices in the securities industry.

Since the 1990s began, each year the NASD has received around 4,000 or more complaints. Each year it expels as many as 40 firms. Each year it bars as many as 490 individuals. Some of the stories behind the stats display incomprehensible outrages, like robbing elderly people of their means of support by pushing them into scary but high-commission investments. What's so alarming is not that such people exist, but that so many of them seem to gravitate to the money game.

CHAPTER 10

The Spoiler: Health Care

If it's your destiny to be rich, young, and retired, it is also in the cards that you will be paying more out of your own pocket for your health care insurance than you ever dreamed possible. The simple fact is that health care costs are so badly out of control that something has to be done to rein them in within the next few years. And universal coverage, following the megacrash of the Clinton reform plan, seems dead for the foreseeable future. So it is inevitable that affluent older people are going to have to pay more, maybe a lot more. Count on it. And plan for it. As Representative Bill Thomas, chairman of the Health Care Subcommittee of the House Ways and Means Committee, put it not long ago: "The free ride is over."

Let's take a minute now to review the complicated but critical facts of this situation. Then we'll offer some guidance.

What Representative Thomas is talking about is this: The

consumer—you and your family—has been largely shielded from the increasingly unbearable bill for health care costs. The government and your employer have been paying, and bleeding as a result. If current U.S. trends continue, over the next decade total medical spending will spike to more than $2.1 trillion annually, more than double the current figure. In part that is because of federal medical entitlements: the cost of Medicare, which covers about 75% of medical costs for 96% of the nation's 34.4 million seniors, is now $158 billion and rising by 8% to 9% annually—more than double the inflation rate. At this rate, the system will be bankrupt in less than a decade, by 2002.

On the private front, the situation is far more positive. To stem spiraling costs, companies have pushed their employees from traditional fee-for-service medicine, in which you choose your own doctors, into managed-care networks. As a result, private employers have been spending less on health care than they used to, a staggering accomplishment when compared to the public sector, where costs are out of control. But even private-sector costs are so huge that efforts to trim will continue, with particular emphasis on retirees, whose doctor and hospital bills dwarf those of young employees.

Even more ominous, most retirees have no experience with managed care. But employers, government officials, and others who are trying to limit health care costs are coaxing seniors into managed-care networks. Within the next few years the coaxing may get more demanding, and retirees may be forced into such networks as part of a solution to the wild cost spiral of Medicare. But get this: Managed-care operations, such as HMOs (health maintenance organizations), succeed by saving money, and they save money by limiting care. While this is working out among younger people, it has not tested so well among older folks, who need far more—and more costly—attention.

So what does all this mean for future retirees who plan to be financially well off? The experts foresee easier access to health insurance as Congress and state legislatures pass enabling laws. They also predict ever-improving medical care as technology continues to make further stunning breakthroughs. But here's the rub: It will cost more, and there is no guarantee you will be covered if you are not able to pay.

Between now and the end of the century, major changes will have to be made in the overall system of health care in general and in Medicare in particular. No one can predict exactly what the landscape will look like as a result, but anyone contemplating retirement needs to grapple with the following issues. And the earlier you plan to call it quits, the more seriously you will need to take them.

Make sure you're covered for the in-between years before 65. Understandably, few of the optimists who plan early retirements think much at all about this point, but it becomes more important every year. That is because employers are gradually whittling away at benefits for early retirees. A growing minority of corporations, in fact, have either eliminated all health coverage for future early retirees or are considering doing so. And many more are cutting way back in coverage or raising premiums.

If you are contemplating early retirement, then, you will need to build this cost into your plans. The place to do so is in the worksheet in Chapter 4. First you might want to get an idea from your company's benefits department of just how much your health care coverage would be affected by early retirement. If it turns out you'll be on your own, you'll need to figure on paying between $6,000 and $10,000 a year for a couple for medical coverage, depending on the amount of insurance you decide on and on where you live.

At the very least, your employer is required under CO-BRA (Consolidated Omnibus Budget Reconciliation Act of 1986) to allow you to stay in its group health plan for 18 months after you leave the company. You have to pay whatever the company's cost is plus a 2% fee. (The average annual cost to companies for providing medical coverage to retirees runs just under $2,500 for a single and around $5,000 for a couple.)

After the 18 months of COBRA coverage are over, you can usually convert from the company's group plan to an individual plan. These are generally very limited in coverage but do not require a medical examination. You might also shop group plans offered by professional associations you belong to or such groups as the American Association of Retired Persons.

Beyond that, it makes sense to become as sharp a consumer of health care services as you can. For instance, if your employer offers a choice between traditional indemnity coverage and managed care, it pays to at least try the new way. Managed care can save you $500 or more a year in out-of-pocket costs, and if you decide that you like it well enough, you will be better positioned for the future, when managed care will probably be the standard for almost everybody.

Another way to become a good consumer is to get into the habit of shopping for medical services, something Americans have never before been encouraged to do. You'll feel more comfortable about it knowing that studies show that doctors' bills can vary by as much as 250% in the same geographic area. You can call your local medical society or consumer-action group, both of which are listed in the

Yellow Pages, to find out what price surveys are published in your city.

Make a separate assessment of the years after 65. This may be the toughest cost projection you will have to make in planning your retirement, for two reasons.

First, the Medicare program that brings health care insurance to everyone when they reach the age of 65, as previously noted, is headed for bankruptcy, and its fate is in the hands of politicians. So no one can project exactly how things will turn out. But the best estimates available indicate that the better off you are, the more you will have to pay. Deductibles would most likely be raised for those with incomes above, say, $70,000 a year, and so would premiums and copayments.

Second, employers almost always retain the right to modify or cancel medical benefits for retirees. They can and do make adjustments—almost always in their favor—all the time. For instance, most large employers either have changed their retiree medical plans in recent years or plan to do so very soon, according to a major benefits survey.

You will be able to deal with some, but not all, of this exposure through Medigap insurance. This is the coverage created to cover a variety of expenses that Medicare will not pay for. Accordingly, federal law currently provides that insurance companies can offer up to 10 standard Medigap policies, ranging from one that pays only the basic deductibles to one that covers everything from preventive drugs to skilled nursing care. Premiums cover a wide spectrum, too, depending on your age as well as your coverage. Expect to pay anywhere from $300 to more than $800 a year. According to the experts we've talked to, you should sign up for Medigap at age 65 when Medicare kicks in.

There are a couple of ways to lower your Medicare-

Medigap bill, but you have to give up some flexibility in the bargain:

One is Medicare Select, an experimental program that is available in more than a dozen states and will probably be expanded. Under Medicare Select, you buy a supplemental policy that is less expensive than ordinary Medigap policies. But in exchange for the price break, you have to agree to use only those doctors and hospitals that are members of the plan's formal network. If you visit a doctor or hospital outside the network, you are responsible for paying any deductibles or copayments under Medicare.

The other option is to join an HMO that has agreed to take Medicare patients. You may have to pay a premium in addition to your regular Medicare Part B premium. In some cases, joining the HMO brings you a wider range of services plus an emphasis on prevention. But you also have to pay in full for any services you use that are outside the HMO. You won't even get the usual 80% payment from Medicare, because Medicare pays the HMO for taking you in. If you don't like the HMO, you have the option of dropping out with a month's notice.

A cheering note: Some employers provide their retirees with continued coverage even after Medicare starts, in effect giving you very inexpensive Medigap coverage. Those who are so generous often hold out this benefit for you and your spouse, even allowing the spouse to keep the coverage after your death on the understanding that it would be very expensive for him or her to switch to a standard Medigap policy at that late date. If you work for a large corporation, find out if you will get this coverage; if so, you can omit provision for full Medigap premiums later on. If you don't have this coverage, you might take the opportunity to ask your company to lay it on. The suggestion can't hurt.

Become a bit of an expert. Since the exact configuration of the coming world of health care is impossible to predict, the best general advice is to follow the trends and turn yourself into a semistudent of modern medicine. No kidding. It's fascinating because it's fast moving and many biomiracles are in the making.

Cures for Alzheimer's, certain forms of cancer, asthma, and other afflictions may be around the corner. And alternative forms of medicine are showing great promise for older people. *Tai chi* exercise from China and diet-based regimens are only two of them. There's also preventive medicine, which is at the very heart of the belief that HMOs can save money: steer people away from bad health habits and they stay healthier. You'll also be able to avoid expensive treatments that provide little or no benefits. Experts estimate that unneeded medical procedures may account for up to 30% of all procedures.

A last word: You may be wondering whether you should plan for the expense of long-term-care insurance. That is a very important question and one with two plausible sides to it. Because it is central to a related issue—how to keep from outliving your money—we address it in Chapter 15.

CHAPTER 11

How to Choose Your New Hometown

Now for the fun of it all. The hard work and planning that go into a successful early retirement need to be leavened with fantasy. And what could be more satisfying than day-dreaming about the new life you'll be able to start after you retire? And how can you fantasize efficiently if you don't have a place in mind?

Try these images: A tropical island set in a turquoise sea. A New England saltbox within earshot of the Atlantic surf. A view of the Grand Teton range out your kitchen window. A picturebook town in the foothills of the Sierras. An apartment 20 floors up with a sweeping view of the Manhattan skyline. A perch in the Sausalito hills with San Francisco rising from the morning fog. A seventeenth-century Tuscan farmhouse.

Only a clod with a heavily challenged imagination could be unmoved. If that description fits you, it's a pity. Maybe this chapter will help. If you're romantically inclined about places, though, this chapter will bring a little direction to your dreams.

So let's get real right now: Four out of five retirees don't move anywhere. They stay put among the sweet memories of their working and parenting lives. Some of them find adventure in travel. Others don't need the shock of the new to live happily ever after. But there are signs that this may be changing.

There's the economic reason: As life gets more and more expensive, it is less and less possible for two people to remain living in four- and five-bedroom houses worth a fortune that could be put to better use.

There's the tax reason: Every year, more people move from one state (or city or country) to another to get away from high taxes. When a typical middle-class family earning $79,000 a year can go from paying $10,500 in state and local taxes in New York to $2,300 in Alaska, as a recent **MONEY** magazine study showed, the incentive is there.

And there's the generational reason: Americans have become more and more willing to pull up stakes and move for jobs. As the great baby boom generation prepares for retirement, experts see reason to expect that fewer and fewer retirees will elect to stay where duty has kept them. You can hear them now: "Maybe retirement used to mean rest. But now it means a new life. Freedom at last!"

The great question addressed in this chapter is this: "How will I know where I'll be happiest in retirement?" This is no simple question, because most people are unaware of their preferences in places to live until they are tested.

Here are the general categories of places you may want to pick. If you can, you might try to identify the type of location that will be best for you. It goes like this:

City. If you live in a big city, you know the dynamic: you trade off high costs, crime, noise, anonymity, and other deterrents for an array of cultural excitements. If you live elsewhere and are pining for the big town, you had better get a dose of total immersion—living in one for more than a week or two—before committing yourself. Surprises will abound.

Country. The trade-offs are just the reverse: low costs for crime, noise; more friendliness, but quiet that can drive some people bonkers.

Retirement community. Plenty of security and people your own age, but age segregation, low energy, and a sameness in so many aspects of life—from what you do to the house you occupy.

College community. Lots of intellectual activity and recreation, but sometimes youthful exuberance can seem maniacally out of control to older people.

These four alternatives are painted in extremes here to make the point that only by experiencing the day-to-day reality of a place will you be able to make up your mind about it. Only, for example, by living in Manhattan, or San Francisco, or Paris will you know whether the pulsating urban energy lifts you up or tears you down.

For this reason experts suggest that you might make a game out of evaluating places—one that can go on for decades as you move closer to retirement. Every time you take a vacation, ask yourself if you might like living in a place like this.

As you zero in on one or two places, try to spend a total of six months to a year making long visits to your spot (in all four seasons, if possible). Meet the people who may become your neighbors, shop in local stores and eat in the community's restaurants, try out the recreational facilities, read the local paper and get a sense of local politics. One of the most important considerations of all: See if you and the weather agree. If you wonder why Florida and California are the most popular states for Americans who retire, that's the reason; lots of warm sun can make up for lots of deprivations. In fact, most lists of the most popular retirement states find that the majority of the top 10 entries are Sunbelt states. Outside of the South and Southwest, the most popular states are Pennsylvania, New Jersey, and Washington State.

Not long ago **MONEY** magazine assembled a panel of seven experts to help choose the top 20 retirement locations in America. We started with an expert consensus on the seven characteristics that retirees would be looking for in a retirement place. The seven, beginning with the most important, are: a low crime rate, mild climate, affordable housing, attractive environment, proximity to cultural and educational activities, strong economic outlook, and excellent health care. Then the experts ranked the 20 U.S. spots that best answered these demands.

Here are the 20 towns and the reasons they stood out:

1. PRESCOTT, ARIZONA (pop. 28,211)

This mile-high mountain town wins top billing for its combination of outstanding physical attributes. The town center retains an Old West flavor. The weather is mild and moderately dry year round (with temperature highs in the summer that rarely exceed 85 degrees and in the winter that average around 50 degrees; humidity stays at a steady 45% year round). The air is clean and the surrounding environment gorgeous, with mountain backdrops and a bordering national forest of 1.25 million acres.

Outdoorsiness seems to keep retirees young here. With 300 sunny days a year, you can play golf and tennis just about daily. Prescott's 900 acres of city parks include nine softball fields. Nearby Granite Mountain Wilderness area offers 7,600 feet for rock climbing. Culture rears its brainy head with four museums and three small peforming arts facilities. A local college offers seniors hundreds of courses at low fees. And if this isn't enough, Phoenix is only 90 miles away.

Principal drawback: It's not cheap. The average cost of a two-bedroom house or condo is $115,000, and average property tax is $1,000 a year. And those with strong cosmopolitan tastes may find the choices here, from restaurants to movies, somewhat limited.

2. FAIRHOPE, ALABAMA (pop. 9,000)

This is the kind of town that fairly drips with Southern charm, has very affordable housing and a booming arts scene, and is close enough to several big cities to seem both small and not forgotten. Some particulars: Fairhope is set on the eastern shore of Mobile Bay amid huge live oaks and Spanish moss. Flower baskets hang from streetlights and telephone poles, and each year up to 250 new trees are planted along tiny Fairhope's streets and in its parks. It's easy to envision yourself occupying one of the serene old homes overlooking the bay. While a three- or four-bedroom house in such a prime spot might fetch $500,000, prices for a two-bedroom house or condo average only $80,000.

For a small Southern town, Fairhope is notably open-hearted (with a pride in its warm welcome for newcomers) and open-minded (with its complement of artists and writers). Its Eastern Shore Arts Center offers classes in painting, figure drawing, and pottery taught by local residents. Fairhope's annual arts and crafts festival attracts more than 450 exhibitors from fully half the states. And violent crime is nearly nonexistent.

Principal drawback: The price to be paid for flowers that bloom year round (average temperature in winter: 60 degrees) is Fairhope's 66 inches of annual rainfall. The drenching humidity swings above 90% in the summer. If you revel in high, dry mountain climes, Fairhope, with all its assets, is not for you.

3. MOUNT DORA, FLORIDA (pop. 7,500)

This is one of those surprises that you fall in love with. Mount Dora is a New England village nestled in the hills of central Florida overlooking six-mile-long Lake Dora. In short, Mount Dora shouldn't be where it is, but what a pleasure to find it there, away from both the nasty New England winters and the dreary flatness that is much of Florida. And Mount Dora bears up very well under close scrutiny.

Downtown is studded with landmark buildings and friendly little shops. The town is laced with leafy parks and neighborhoods that boast an abundance of attractive, affordable homes in a variety of styles. Aside from the colonial, Victorian, and Spanish representation, there is the special charm of 1920s cracker-style houses with wraparound porches, clapboard siding, and tin roofs. You'll pay $70,000 or so for an average two-bedroom house or condo, and a three-bedroom spread on Lake Dora may set you back $250,000 or more. It's only 25 miles to Orlando, but you might not get bored in the town that's called Festival City. The biggest is the annual arts festival in February, drawing 200,000 visitors. There's even a resident theater company that stages three or four productions a year.

Principal drawbacks: Hard to say, unless you think that a town half of whose residents are retired is a little too homogeneous for you.

4. LAS VEGAS, NEVADA (pop. 920,000)

Escape. That's the word that most easily sums up the phenomenon that is Las Vegas. The town was built on the promise of escape into a fantastic, endless-night world of gambling casinos. Now it has become the fastest-growing city in the nation and double its size of a decade ago, as Californians, many of them retirees, flee their own state's high taxes, sagging economy, and social stresses.

What they find in Nevada is no state income tax, some of the lowest property taxes in the country, and dry, clean desert air that bursts with sunlight 293 days out of the year. And to accommodate the armies of retirees there is an ongoing boom in residential construction. The average cost of a two-bedroom house or condo runs to $115,000, with most new homes located in planned communities with all the amenities from tennis courts to swimming pools to shopping centers, sometimes even to libraries.

If you like planned communities, you will probably find the state of the art in Vegas—like Summerlin, a 22,000-acre expanse that even enfolds one of the Del Webb Sun City subdivisions, where attractive, desert-architecture homes fetch from $92,000 to $240,000. Sun City Las Vegas alone has two 18-hole golf courses; Las Vegas overall has nearly two dozen golf courses, with more planned. And of course there's the strip, where you can lose all your money but save by chowing down on the $3.99 buffets with unlimited choice of food.

Principal drawbacks: Summer, when even a lack of humidity can't make up for temperatures that punch way above the 100-degree mark. Crime, which has cooled down but still achieves a rate in Vegas that ranks among the worst third of the cities surveyed by the FBI. Traffic congestion, an unavoidable by-product of a furious growth rate.

5. CHAPEL HILL, NORTH CAROLINA (pop. 42,000)

The trend toward retiring in a college town is one of those powerful mass impulses that also happens to be sound. Typical of life's many pleasures that are served up in college towns: tons of cultural activities, scads of cut-rate classes to attend, oceans of youthful energy to partake in, and an abundance of first-rate health care services, thanks to the university-related hospitals there. So if you'd like to put your favorite college town to the test, Chapel Hill is the one to best.

Not only do you get all of the above amenities, you get them roughly in triplicate. That's because Chapel Hill and its University of North Carolina campus anchor one corner of the University Triangle. The other two: Raleigh, 20 miles to the east, which is home to North Carolina State University; and Durham, eight miles to the north, where Duke University is located. You also get Georgian halls of ivy on the university's handsome campus, plus mild winters and summers that are virtually cool for the South. In *Sunbelt Retirement* (Regnery), author Peter A. Dickinson summed up the look of the place perfectly: "Compared to similar university towns, Chapel Hill is quieter than Ann Arbor, cleaner than Berkeley, and quainter than Princeton."

Principal drawbacks: Priciness, particularly when it comes to the area's tight housing market. Houses generally run in the $200,000 to $300,000 range, with smaller two-bedroom houses or condos starting around $100,000. Average property taxes are $1,000 to $1,500.

6. NAPLES, FLORIDA (pop. 19,500)

If you know the Old World better than the New, Naples is misnamed. It's the opposite of the raucous, decaying city in Italy; it's clean, neat, and unrelentingly upscale. In fact, with its canals sporting fine homes at the waterline, it's more like a neo-Venice. (A section of town is actually called Venice and is modeled on the Italian original.) Points of local pride are the Philharmonic Center for the Arts, which attracts top orchestras, dance troupes, and Broadway shows; 40 golf courses; and seven miles of beaches and shoreline for prime fishing, sailing, and snorkeling. Naples has such abundant charm that many people fall in love with the town at first sight. If you admire cunningly gorgeous artifice, you may be among them. And Florida, with no income tax, is one of the kindest states of all in this regard.

Principal drawbacks: Price and congestion. While the average cost of a two-bedroom condo is around $80,000, many homes will run you in the mid or even high six figures. And Naples has undergone heavy growth in the last decade, with the result that getting around town involves all-too-regular traffic hassles.

7. SEDONA, ARIZONA (pop. 7,900)

If you liked the story of our top-ranked town, Prescott, Arizona—outstanding natural beauty and near-perfect weather—you should compare this prize with Sedona, just down the road. The trade-offs: Sedona is a bit warmer in summer and milder in winter than Prescott, which sits at a majestic 5,390 feet above sea level. But at 4,240 feet, Sedona is still far above the harsher desert floor. Instead of Prescott's forest-and-mountain setting, Sedona has the Coconino National Forest and one of the most spectacular natural settings in the world, Oak Creek Canyon. Its fabulous red rock formations have played key supporting roles in generations of Hollywood westerns.

This glory in turn has attracted hundreds of artists to settle in the area, giving the town a Carmel-by-the-Canyon flavor with over 40 art galleries. Sedona's emphasis on the arts (including such events as an annual "Jazz on the Rocks" festival in a natural amphitheater) puts it a bit behind Prescott in the pursuit of other forms of recreation. But its relative sophistication closes the gap. It would be great fun just choosing between these two semiheavenly spots.

Principal drawbacks: Real estate is even pricier than Prescott's. Average cost of a two-bedroom condo or house is $150,000 to $200,000. But some new entries are asking $500,000 and more.

8. PALM SPRINGS, CALIFORNIA (pop. 42,000)

This is an easy one, because you'll probably love it or hate it. If you really warm to Palm Springs, it will be a place with more to do than you can keep up with, weather that is perfect most of the year, and prices that are affordable if

111

you're willing to shop around. If you're turned off, then Palm Springs will be a glitzy, snobby, pricey 'burb that's too crowded, too full of itself, and, contrary to song and story about the winelike high desert breezes, even has occasional bad air.

Both versions of the Palm Springs area are believable, because your idea of a retirement paradise is all a matter of your taste. A clue: If you like city life and resort amenities, including palatial shopping centers and 82 golf courses at last count, you'll go for Palm Springs. But if you're the quiet country type, you won't.

Principal drawbacks: You guessed it. The cost of living stands tall at 19% above the national average, the highest of the 20 towns in our ranking. Housing in the area can of course cost you the stars, which is to be expected when the likes of Bob Hope and Frank Sinatra live there. Average cost of a two-bedroom condo or house: $92,000 to $103,000, a fact that reflects the variety of offerings available.

9. AIKEN, SOUTH CAROLINA (pop. 20,500)

You may be starting to notice that the leading subdivision of this list of top retirement places is what you could call "Most Charming Southern Town." So far, Fairhope, Mount Dora, and Chapel Hill have vied for the title. Each has its special appeal. By any standard, Aiken would be in the running, if only because of its stunning stock of antebellum mansions spared by the Union Army as it pursued its Confederate foes to the sea. The town retains a genteel air of yore, even in many smaller homes set on precise, shaded lawns.

What put modern Aiken on the map was an influx of rich Northerners, starting before the turn of the century, who found its mild climate perfect for wintering and its terrain ideal for raising and training horses. This moneyed equine set brought behind it a range of upscale amenities ranging from abundant golf courses to symphony, dance, theater, and other high-culture pastimes. A large supply of small, modest homes keeps the average price of a two-bedroom house or condo at $40,000 to $80,000. Property taxes are low. But if your taste for Southern towns leans toward the quiet and sedate, socially active Aiken may not be your spot.

Principal drawbacks: None in general. It's all a matter of taste. For instance, some visitors are turned off by the landed-gentry past that lives on in some quarters here. Others either like it or take no notice.

10. FAYETTEVILLE, ARKANSAS (pop. 43,000)

First off, Fayetteville is not in the running for "Most Charming Southern Town." Its allure is real but far from precious: mild climate with cooler summers than most of Arkansas; low housing prices and the lowest cost of living of our 20 spots; and educational, recreational, and cultural opportunities that leave a lot of the prettier places in the dust. This is because Fayetteville is a college town, home of the University of Arkansas. Tourist stops like Eureka Springs are nearby. Fayetteville itself abounds with senior groups and medical services.

Principal drawbacks: The low cost of living reflects the fact that Arkansas is one of the poorest states, so don't look for the kind of consumer-goods abundance you may more readily find elsewhere. And the nearest big city is Tulsa, a tiring 115 miles away.

11. KERRVILLE, TEXAS (pop. 18,000)

This town is the pick of the Texas hill country, which for many connoisseurs of places is the pick of Texas. The lake-dotted, live-oak-and-pine-filled scenery is matched by some of the best weather in the United States, with temperatures averaging around 80 in summer and the high forties in winter. An artists' colony is building in Kerrville, and the presence of the Cowboy Artists of America Museum attests to it. In addition, the Hill Country Arts Foundation provides arts and crafts instruction, and the Kerrville Performing Arts Society draws nationally recognized performers. Kerrville State Park offers 500 acres for everything from camping to hiking to swimming. What's more, the cost of living runs 6% below the national average, the average two-bedroom house or condo costs from $60,000 to $80,000, and Texas has no income tax. Charming San Antonio lies a mere 60 miles away.

Principal drawbacks: None, unless you're either a taxophile or a Texaphobe.

12. BREVARD, NORTH CAROLINA (pop. 5,500)

Like Sedona, this town is in that special class of places surrounded by rare natural beauty. This time it's some of the best of the Appalachians, with stretches of the Blue Ridge and the Great Smokies close by. In Brevard's very backyard is the Pisgah National Forest, with 200 miles of trout streams, 300 miles of hiking trails, and more than 200 waterfalls. Mean temperatures are in the low forties in winter and the low seventies in summer, considerably more bearable than other parts of the state. Culture is a presence, too, led by the Brevard Music Center, which attracts world-class musicians for opera, concerts, and musicals during the summer.

Principal drawbacks: Living is not cheap. While the average two-bedroom house or condo costs $68,000 to $95,000, land is relatively expensive, and some newer homes top the half-million-dollar mark, a rarity in this state.

13. DURANGO, COLORADO (pop. 13,000)

Now we're back to the Western version of knock-your-socks-off natural beauty. This time it's the really high (peaks up to 14,000 feet) San Juan range of the Rockies. This ruggedness is the backdrop for a town that has managed to hold on to much of its Victorian character while at the same time undergoing a latter-day version of the kind of growth that put Aspen and Vail on the map. With the growth has come the expected goods and services—some fine shops and ambitious chefs have moved into town. The local Fort Lewis College offers a wide range of noncredit classes and puts on six theater productions a year. That's in addition to Durango's own community theater. Dominating a plethora of outdoor opportunities is the Purgatory Ski Resort 25 miles to the north, with its 70 trails and nine lifts.

Principal drawbacks: As you might expect, Durango has been getting expensive as it has grown. Population is up 15% in two years, and house prices spurted 21% in 1994 alone. The average two-bedroom house or condo costs $80,000 to $110,000. The nearest big city, Albuquerque, is 215 rocky miles away.

14. ASHEVILLE, NORTH CAROLINA (pop. 64,000)

Asheville is the city version of number 12, Brevard. What Asheville offers that Brevard doesn't is real urban life. It is the true capital of western North Carolina, with services and amenities that rival those of larger cities. Its medical facilities are particularly rich, and it has a branch of the University of North Carolina. Seniors are particularly well served by these and other institutions. And Ashville is one of those Southern cities that has held on to its beauty.

Principal drawbacks: As in Brevard, living is costly. And since Asheville is a real city, it cannot claim the safety that the smaller towns in this ranking enjoy.

15. MYRTLE BEACH, SOUTH CAROLINA (pop. 26,000)

This is the single ocean location in our ranking. Its major appeal is to those for whom there is nothing to match the roar of the surf and the crunch of sand under bare feet. Today Myrtle Beach offers much more, so those who recoil from the summer throngs might look elsewhere. What they'll miss is the pride of this area, the Grand Strand and its 60 miles of beaches backed up by some 80 golf courses and innumerable resorts and condo developments. With all this growth, however, the cost of living still is about 5% below the national average, the average two-bedroom house or condo costs $70,000 to $85,000, and property taxes are reasonable.

Principal drawbacks: The traditional summer crowds that used to disappear after Labor Day, leaving retirees in peace, have begun showing up all year long. They're attracted by a country-and-western entertainment scene similar to that in Nashville and Branson, Missouri. As a result, Myrtle Beach has become one of the top three tourist destinations in the United States.

16. ST. GEORGE, UTAH (pop. 38,000)

For outdoors devotees who go especially for mountain and desert, it's hard to do better than this. St. George backs into Zion National Park, a place that, once visited, is never forgotten for its geologically extravagant beauty. The area's four-season climate is dry and affords fine winter skiing close by. The city of St. George, with its backdrop of sheer red cliffs and its pleasant leafy streets, offers more variety than most spots in the intermountain West. There is a celebrity concert series as well as ballet, opera, and sports events at the town's Dixie Center; and there's legal gambling in nearby Mesquite, Nevada. St. George's sizable population, perhaps 25% retirees, has been swelled by newcomers in recent years, adding variety to this heavily Mormon town.

Principal drawbacks: Relative remoteness (the closest big city is Las Vegas, 120 miles away).

17. HENDERSONVILLE, NORTH CAROLINA (pop. 7,500)

This town, along with Brevard and Asheville, forms a compact triangle in northwest North Carolina. Much of what we could say about Hendersonville has already been noted about the other two. While Hendersonville shares Brevard's small-town flavor, it can't quite compete with that town's gorgeous surrounding countryside. But Hendersonville's slightly bigger size brings with it additional amenities, in-

117

cluding the Flat Rock Playhouse, widely considered one of the top summer stock theaters in the United States.

Principal drawbacks: Same as Brevard and Asheville: cost of living.

18. SEQUIM, WASHINGTON (pop. 4,100)

This is our lone offering in the northwest United States, which may seem surprising given all the people who have been migrating there in recent years. While this part of the country has many fine towns, great natural beauty, and an increasing range of cultural attractions, the choicest coastal areas tend to be wetter than most retirees would like. But Sequim is different, resting as it does in the dry shadow of the mighty Olympic Mountains. So Sequim (pronounced "Squim") has only about 16 inches of rain a year, compared with 50 for Seattle and even more elsewhere in the state. With the Olympics as a backdrop and the Strait of Juan de Fuca on your doorstep, the hunting, fishing, hiking, and birdwatching opportunities abound. If you like this area, with its fresh and invigorating climate (average year-round high temperature is about 45 degrees, with summer highs in the mid-seventies), you might want to look also at the neighboring towns of Port Angeles and Port Townsend, where rainfall is a bit higher but excellent opportunities for retirees exist too. Washington is an income-tax-free state.

Principal drawbacks: Sequim has the highest proportion of retirees on our list—52% of the town's population. While fine for some, it doesn't sit well with seniors who want a more cosmopolitan mix. Housing costs can run on the high side, a reflection of how popular this town has become. Average cost of a two-bedroom house or condo: $120,000.

19. CHARLESTON, SOUTH CAROLINA (pop. 83,000)

This and Las Vegas are the only two real cities in our ranking. In every other way, though, they are truly a continent apart. While Vegas is wild, flashy, and growing like a hormone-drenched adolescent, Charleston is steeped in history and rooted in an aristocratic tradition where movement is slow and stately. And culture is as thick as the air on an August afternoon. Start with 32 annual festivals headed by Spoleto U.S.A., a 17-day international performance and visual arts event in late May and early June. Then there's Worldfest Charleston, an international film festival in November. There are nine museums, scores of historic houses in town, and numerous plantations in the countryside. And a vibrant restaurant scene marks Charleston as one of the only Southern cities outside New Orleans with long-standing culinary credentials. Housing, considering Charleston's architectural heritage, is not expensive, with two–bedroom condos and houses averaging $85,000 to $110,000.

Principal drawbacks: Sultry summers with temperature highs in the nineties. And while there are plenty of services for seniors, it is not as easy as many other places for outsiders to get accepted.

20. CLAYTON, GEORGIA (pop. 1,600)

This is the smallest of our top towns and, because of its size and location in the mountains of north Georgia, in some ways the most remote. (Greenville, S.C., 86 miles away, is the closest city.) To some connoisseurs of retirement places, Clayton is also the prettiest. One expert even describes it as "precious," with its requisite fine old houses set on deep lawns with lush flora everywhere. It's hard by

119

two big lakes and only six miles to a ski lift. "Ski in winter, water ski in summer," says Robert Tillman, producer of the *Retirement in America* video series. Clemsom University is an easy drive, and there are several state colleges in the region. If you worry that outsiders might be shunned in such a tiny country town, it might help to know that a third of Clayton's retirees are from elsewhere. Cost of living runs 7% to 10% below the national figure; and a two-bedroom house or condo averages a modest $80,000 to $87,000.

Principal drawbacks: Sixty inches or more of rainfall a year. Otherwise no drawbacks, if a rural tempo and culture give you joy.

If these choices aren't enough to fantasize about, the next chapter will fling you into the deepest and most romantic distances of all: if, where, when, and how to retire abroad.

CHAPTER 12

The Ultimate Fantasy: Retiring Abroad

This is a specialized dream: it's made only for the favored few who harbor a spirit of adventure so robust that the thrill of living in an alien culture makes them forget the comforts of home. Sure, it's fun to imagine yourself living on an ancient cobblestoned street on Paris's Left Bank. Or tramping the rugged Irish coast in your tweeds. Or directing a houseful of servants from your poolside perch in Cuernavaca. But those are only surface snapshots of the expatriate life. So be warned:

1. You are probably not among the favored few who can thrive abroad.
2. If you think you are, you must prove it by rigorously testing yourself in the foreign place of choice.
3. If you move there before giving the place—and yourself—a thorough vetting, you will almost surely be unhappy.

With all the obstacles, then, you might well ask yourself why thousands of retired Americans gleefully scatter themselves to all corners of the globe. It's the possibilities, really. Two stand out:

1. You feel superalive and hyperaware living day to day in a foreign environment: yes, strangeness can be exhilarating.
2. Living abroad gives you the chance of a comfortable, sometimes luxurious existence on a fraction of what it would cost you stateside.

If you're interested, "go see for yourself," urges Jane Parker, coauthor with Allene Symons of *Adventures Abroad: Exploring the Travel/Retirement Option* (Gateway Books, $12.95; 800-669-0773). She suggests that you investigate at least two or three places and start by seeing how they measure up against a basic checklist, including temperate climate, ease of access from the United States, good medical services, moderate- or low-cost housing, Americans in residence there, acceptance of Americans by residents, and, of course, economic and political stability.

Among the spots she and other experts on foreign retirement places favor for Americans: **Costa Rica, Honduras, Ireland, Portugal, and Uruguay.** These are the countries where, according to Parker, you can live for a third to a half of what you would pay for a comparable lifestyle in the United States. For instance, she estimates that at the upper end of the expense spectrum, you can live well in Portugal on $2,000 to $2,200 a month. Mexico would cost you only $1,000 to $1,200 a month and Costa Rica a bit more. Honduras is the bargain basement of this lot. Parker says it's "like Costa Rica 20 years ago, with very inexpensive resort living."

Special note for early retirees: A sojourn in one of these countries has turned out to be a godsend for some people who found themselves, voluntarily or otherwise, retiring well before Social Security and Medicare became available. Moving to a low-cost locale often makes it possible to keep from eating too deeply into your limited retirement savings. On top of that, there are many job opportunities in these places, particularly for those with expertise in computers, banking, accounting, and corporate management. Not only does such work relieve the boredom that can set in among young retirees, but it allows you to shore up your savings and, if you want to, return to the United States in time to claim your Social Security at 62 and your Medicare at 65. (While you can have your Social Security check mailed to you abroad, Medicare coverage does not extend beyond U.S. borders.)

Thinking about retiring abroad? Consider these three basic caveats:

• *Do all your lifestyle homework—and then thorough fieldwork.* Make a list of what you want in a retirement place. What kind of weather? If the tropics or resort living leaves you cold, what are you doing looking at Honduras, for instance? If more than a bit of rain gets you down, cross Ireland from your list. Some places may not have the kind of health care facilities you require but may have helicopter evacuation services to top-notch hospital centers that are almost as good.

Once you have read up on a place, the fieldwork will be more informed. But that doesn't mean you can cut corners. You still should visit an area several times, even if you intend to retire there only part-time. That's the only way to see how the locals treat you and how you respond to their brand of hospitality—and, of course, how you react to the food, the water, the light, and a host of things you won't even think of until you get there. You can get a free packet of information about life in most of the places mentioned from Lifestyle Explorations (508-371-4814). This and other outfits operate pre-retiree tours to some of the most popular countries.

• *Uncover any tax penalties.* For starters, you don't escape U.S. taxes by retiring abroad. You do get to earn up to $70,000 a year free of U.S. income tax while residing abroad. But this break does not apply to investment income, pensions, or annuities—only to earned income. But many countries have higher income taxes than does the United States, a fact that can catch you in an expensive bind. You will need to find out what sort of arrangement exists between the United States and the country you will be living in. You may wind up having to pay tax to either of the two countries or to both. Internal Revenue Service Publication 901, "U.S. Tax Treaties," is your source for researching agreements with 40 countries. Another valuable item: IRS Publication 593, "Tax Highlights for U.S. Citizens and Residents Going Abroad." (You can get free copies of both publications by calling 800-829-3676.)

• *Take a short foreign exchange course.* The plunge of the dollar against other major currencies has been so extreme lately that it has hit the front pages of local newspapers. This has made many Americans aware of currency fluctuations for the first time. But only when you're on the ground in, say, Germany, France, or Japan do you feel the wildly expensive reality of the situation. For instance, if you had retired to France in 1985, you would have been able to buy 20 francs for a dollar. That alone might have persuaded many a francophilic Yank to pack up for Paris. But three years later the dollar fetched only 5.5 francs, and it has been lower since then. In effect, your cost of living would have doubled.

Similarly, a series of Mexican peso devaluations have severely hurt many Americans retired there who made the mistake of putting their assets in pesos. The moral of these tales is not wholly satisfying: No matter how low the greenback gets against other currencies, keep your money in dollars. After all, you can come home again.

CHAPTER 13

How to Handle the Biggest Wad You'll Ever Own

Talk about defining moments. The day will come when you are confronted with one of the greatest single responsibilities of your life. You will be told by your employer just how much your retirement will be worth. There will be your 401(k) and other company savings plans, which will be available as a lump sum. And if you're really lucky, there will be a standard pension, which traditionally is doled out in monthly checks until the end of your life. This is the annuity approach.

But more and more, particularly among larger companies, you are given the option of taking this pension as a lump sum too. So don't be surprised if you are suddenly expected to make some heavy decisions involving a stash amounting to $1 million or more. Will you be ready to do the smart thing? If not, you could be stumbling into the biggest fiasco in your life.

Here are two absolutely essential questions that you'll need to answer when the time comes:

1. *Should I take my pension as a lump sum or an annuity—that is, a check a month for life?*
2. *Should I roll my money over into an IRA or pay tax on it right away at a favorable rate?*

Now let's see what's at stake and just how you should proceed.

Lump Sum or Annuity?

Think about it: You receive a huge wad of cash that must finance the rest of your—and maybe your spouse's—life, and you alone are responsible for investing it all. If the very idea frightens you, that may be the most eloquent argument in favor of choosing an annuity instead of a lump sum. Even if you know a fair amount about personal finance and have been a reasonably successful investor for years, being out there on your own is different when you don't have a regular job to fall back on. And if you feel trepidation now, isn't it likely that after you're retired and have less to occupy your mind, you'll worry even more? Maybe not be able to sleep well some nights when the stock or bond market is misbehaving? And you might wonder how meticulous you will be, as you get on in years, in tending your portfolio. In short, the best thing about an annuity is peace of mind. Period.

The worst thing about an annuity is just as simply stated: It doesn't keep up with inflation. Even Social Security gives you a cost-of-living raise every year (unless, of course, the cost of living doesn't go up). And that's where the unquestioned charm of the lump sum comes in.

But before you make a lunge for a lump, a little examination of conscience is in order. Is it true that the very size of the sum makes you feel invincible? As if you could never run out of money with a cache that humongous? Or are you moved by the warming thought of living off the returns of your lump sum and then being able to leave most or even all of it to your children or grandchildren? If either of these emotions flood your being when you contemplate grabbing for a lump sum, you had better back off and think this thing through.

Yes, it's perfectly understandable that you'd be impressed with the size of a lump sum and yearning to pass it on to your progeny. But these emotions often make for poor logic and really rotten finance. They may mean that you are willing to fudge the one vital question within the lump-or-annuity question itself: *Will taking the lump sum serve your retirement finances better than taking the annuity?*

An important recent development makes this an even more pressing question than ever. When Congress passed legislation in 1994 implementing the GATT treaty on world trade, a provision was quietly inserted in the law that has nothing to do with tariffs but plenty to do with pensions that are taken as lump sums. Under the new law, employers will have to switch to higher interest rate and life-expectancy assumptions in computing their so-called defined-benefit pensions that are distributed as lump sums. This will have the effect of significantly reducing the size of lump-sum payouts, particularly for employees who are now a number of years from retirement. The result, according to experts who have worked out the numbers, could reduce lump-sum pensions as much as 30% to 60% for many workers now in their thirties and forties. Companies are free to make the switch in assumptions when they want, provided it is completed by the year 2000.

When your company's human resources people give you all the relevant numbers just before retirement, you will likely be asked to choose between a lump sum and several annuity alternatives. The single-life figure will be the the highest, of course, since it covers only you. And you'll have to get your spouse to waive his or her rights to your pension if you decide to take the single-life option.

Then there's the joint-and-survivor annuity, which keeps on paying out to your spouse after you die, generally in amounts ranging from 50% to 100% of what you might have been getting. Of course, the more the survivor gets, the less your monthly check is going to be from the start.

Caveat: Insurance companies have a neat retirement-planning device that sounds a lot better than it is. The idea is to go ahead and take the single annuity and its larger monthly paycheck and to use part of the difference to buy a life insurance policy on your life, which protects your spouse. But experts largely disdain this approach, advising you to take the joint annuity. Not only is it safer, but a couple taking the life-insurance route runs the risk of not being able to afford maintaining coverage large enough to provide the income protection a spouse might need.

When trying to make up your mind, remember that your 401(k) will come to you in a lump sum. So if you choose to take your pension as an annuity, that can serve as the income portion of your portfolio, while the 401(k) lump becomes the growth and inflation-protection part.

So let's say you believe you are competent to handle your huge nest egg yourself, or perhaps you have an experienced and trustworthy adviser who can do it for you. In this case, you can confidently consider taking the lump. You can act to protect the value of the sum from inflation by investing it in growth stock funds. You certainly can't do that with an annuity check. Besides, you can get at the principal anytime you need to if emergencies arise or if, say, you decide you have more than enough for yourself and want to start giving something to your heirs.

Here is a very rough rule of thumb you can use to give you an idea if the lump sum is a good deal: Ask your company's benefits department what the effective interest rate is on your pension when taken as an annuity. If the rate is lower than the rate of 30-year Treasury bonds, you would be better off taking the lump sum and buying Treasuries. But if the interest rate on the pension is higher than the Treasury bond rate, you would do well to take the annuity.

This is not to say you should rely solely on the rule of thumb when deciding between a lump sum and an annuity. In any case, it is imperative—repeat, *imperative*—that you get professional help at this time. An experienced tax accountant or retirement planner has the know-how and the software needed to run the numbers both ways and make the technical evaluations needed to come to an informed judgment.

For instance, do you seriously think you can competently crunch all these factors: an annuity income, its implied interest rate, inflation effects over 30 or so years; and, on the other hand, a lump-sum amount with its implied interest rate and a reasonable return on that money; *plus* how well both alternatives fit with the rest of your assets? You would have to be familiar with complicated actuarial assumptions and truly mind-numbing tax rules. (The following section on income averaging versus rollovers will give you some idea of our tax point.)

Double caveat: As pointed out in Chapter 9, "Getting the Right Kind of Help," lump sums are the late-twentieth-century equivalent to the old-fashioned inheritance, which every crook in the kingdom schemed to get his hands on.

Just to give you an idea of the dimensions of the allure, each year lump-sum distributions worth an estimated $100 billion to $125 billion are made in the United States. Insurance salesmen, stockbrokers, financial planners, and accountants are the principal pros who will be swarming around your fortune. You can help yourself immensely or hurt yourself irretrievably in your selection of a financial adviser, especially at this critical period. So if you're having trouble remembering the main points made in Chapter 9, now may be the time for a quick review.

Averaging or Rollover IRA?

If you decide to go for the lump, you're immediately catapulted into another either/or decision. Sorry about that. But this one makes a huge difference in how your money will be taxed. You can choose to take the money and pay tax on it right away, using a highly favorable tax-cutting scheme called **special averaging.** Or you can roll the money over into an IRA and avoid tax on it until you begin taking it out. Both ways have advantages and disadvantages, which we will cover in this section.

Warning: The law is draconian on exactly how you handle the money at the time it is paid out: If you go the IRA route but fail to roll over your money into an IRA within 60 days of receiving it, you are immediately liable to payment of taxes on it. And you have to be extra careful in how the rollover is made. As strong as the impulse may be to hold that much in your hands just for an hour or so, resist it. Instead you should let your company perform the rollover to the brokerage house, mutual fund company,

131

bank, or insurance company of your choice. Otherwise your employer will have to withhold 20% of the wad before handing it over to you. That 20% comes back to you only after you claim a credit for it on your next annual tax return. And that's a hassle and a half.

Now let's take a look at the two methods and then evaluate them.

Averaging

Five- or 10-year averaging allows you to figure your tax as if you had received your lump sum over a five- or 10-year period. Spreading out the amount in this fashion drops you into lower brackets than you otherwise would have to face. But to gain entry into the averaging enclosure, your lump-sum distribution must pass all of the following four tests:

1. It must be from a qualified pension, profit-sharing, stock bonus, or Keogh plan you participated in for at least five years. Ask your plan administrator at work if your company's plan qualifies.
2. It must consist of the entire balance due you from all of your employer's plans.
3. It must be paid to you within a single tax year. Say you retire in March and pay your taxes on a calendar-year basis: then you must receive your entire balance by December 31 of that year.
4. It must be paid after you turn 59½. (If you were born before January 1, 1936, however, this rule does not apply.)

If you square with these requirements, you can apply averaging to the taxable portion of your lump sum: your own nondeductible contributions are not taxable since they were made with your own after-tax dollars; but all your employer's contributions to your account plus its earnings through the years are taxable to you. Your employer will issue you a Form 1099-R, and you will find the taxable amount listed there.

You might want your accountant to figure your tax if you use averaging, but it isn't at all complicated if you want to have a go at it yourself. First you divide the amount by five (as you'll see, this is becoming the more generally used method). For instance, say your lump sum amounts to $200,000, not counting any nondeductible contributions of yours. In this case the whole $200,000 is taxable. With five-year averaging, one-fifth of the total is $40,000. Then you find the tax on that amount, using the rates for single tax-payers. (These are listed in the IRS instruction booklet for filing your annual tax return.) You will probably wind up saving as much as half the tax you otherwise would have to pay without averaging.

You are allowed to use 10-year averaging if you were born before 1936. You figure it the same way you would five-year averaging except that you divide and multiply by 10 instead of five. One major difference: If you use the 10-year method, you will have to use the higher and more steeply graduated 1986 tax rates for singles, which range from 11% to as high as 50%. Current rates run from 15% to 39.6%. In case you qualify for both five- and 10-year averaging, get IRS Form 4972, which you can use to compute your tax both ways and find out which one will save you more.

Since you can use averaging only once in your life, you might want to compare the averaging results with the tax you would pay if you didn't bother to use averaging at all. If the difference is not large and you are a number of years away from leaving work completely, consider paying the regular tax and saving the averaging privilege for a bigger lump sum you may be destined to receive sometime in the future.

Before going on to IRA rollovers, there are two special (and very rare) IRS averaging breaks that you should know about.

The first one, known as the **minimum-distribution allowance,** is nothing short of startling. If your lump sum is less than $70,000, part of it is tax-free. Half of the first $20,000 is exempt. Above that amount, the tax-free element phases out. At $30,000, $8,000 is tax-free; at $40,000, it's $6,000; at $50,000, it's $4,000; at $60,000, it's $2,000; and at $70,000 or more, the exemption is zero.

The second averaging break allows you lower taxation if you were born before January 1, 1936, and earned some of your retirement benefits before 1974. Then part of your distribution can be treated as a capital gain, with a favorable 20% tax rate. Compare that to current income tax rates of up to 39.6% and to the top capital-gains rate of 28%. If you think you qualify for this break, ask your employer to tell you how much of your stash is favored.

Rollovers
IRA rollovers permit you to postpone paying any tax on your lump sum until you withdraw it. You can put your money into one, two, or more IRAs, as you like. If you also have a Keogh plan, which you would have set up with earnings from self-employment, you can do a rollover and still reserve your right to five- or 10-year averaging. Here's how you do it: Put your lump-sum distribution into the Keogh; later on, you can take a lump-sum distribution from it and use averaging to compute your tax.

Doing a rollover is simple; you just have to make sure

it's done correctly. Have your employer transfer the money directly to your IRA or IRAs. This avoids having 20% of the payout withheld. And if you're under 59½, you also avoid being nicked for an unrefundable 10% early-withdrawal penalty on the 20% unless you make it up out of your own pocket. Unfortunately, neither your own after-tax contributions to the plan nor any lump-sum severance pay can be included as part of the rollover; these would be considered excess amounts subject to a 6% excise tax.

If you don't want to roll over your total distribution, you can take part of it yourself and pay regular income tax on it (plus the 10% early withdrawal penalty if you're under 59½). But if you make such a split, you can't use averaging. You are required to report a rollover on line 16 of your 1040 for that year. If you omit this information, the IRS will figure you are not reporting regular income and will send you a hefty tax bill.

And the choice is . . . the IRA, usually. Consider this example: A $250,000 distribution was made in 1994 to a 62-year-old retiree in the combined 34% federal and state tax bracket. An annual before-tax return of 6.5% is expected. Ten years later, when the retiree is 72, here are the results. If a rollover IRA had been chosen for the $250,000, no immediate tax would be paid and the accumulated assets by age 72 would be $440,643. With 10-year averaging, $44,118 would be immediately taken away in tax, leaving only $205,882 available for investment. The upshot in 10 years: accumulated assets totaling $300,471.

With five-year averaging, $55,635 would be taxed right away, with only $194,365 available for investment. After 10 years the accumulated assets would amount to $283,663. The IRA rollover wins by a country mile. Of course, when the retiree started withdrawing the money, he or she would

135

have to pay taxes at the regular income tax rate, which could be higher later on. It almost surely would be higher than the reduced rate under averaging.

The wisest thing to do before settling on a rollover would be to ask your accountant or financial planner to figure the current tax on your lump sum using five-year averaging (and 10-year averaging, too, if you qualify). Also have the tax pro make an estimate of the tax you would pay on future distributions from an IRA. Then compare the two, making sure that the pro accounts for the return you will make on the IRA.

Even if the IRA wins out on all counts, there are times when people need large amounts of cash right away. For instance, you may want to start a new business. Then by all means use the averaging method. Even though it may not save you as much in taxes as an IRA, it is a prudent compromise.

CHAPTER 14

The Lowdown on Variable Annuities

There is one approach to investing that we have not mentioned at all up to this point: **variable annuities.** Our intent was not to deceive, but to simplify. The truth is that many people reading this book will never need to consider this alternative. And no one who has not made *full use* of the tax-deferred alternatives we have been talking about—401(k)s, 403(b)s, IRAs, Keoghs—should be thinking about variable annuities. With this unbendable proviso, then, who should be considering these complicated investments? Here's who:

Variable annuities, essentially tax-deferred mutual funds, can be valuable investment tools for people in the 28% tax bracket or higher (1995 taxable income above $39,000 for couples and above $23,400 for singles) who are willing to keep their hands off their money for at least 10 years.

This chapter will give you all you need to know to be an intelligent buyer of these increasingly popular products. Variable annuities are investment packages that contain two elements: a life insurance guarantee plus mutual funds that offer the potential for big tax-deferred capital gains. But you'll see why we insist that you fully fund your 401(k) or similar plan before turning to variables.

Aside from their insurance element, which you may or may not welcome, variables are inferior to 401(k)-like accounts for two main reasons. First, instead of being able to buy them with plump before-tax dollars, you must use after-tax dollars. Second, variables come festooned with fees, including stiff surrender charges that run as high as 9% of principal if you decide to drop out within the first seven to 10 years of ownership.

So what's to love about them? Again, two things. First, the returns that build up inside the annuity are tax-deferred until you start getting a payout, just as with IRAs, Keoghs, and 401(k)s. Second—and a sizable advantage over those plans—you can stash as much as you want in variables. That's right, there are absolutely no limits to what you can put into a variable annuity. In this sense it's potentially the biggest tax shelter you could find.

Just as with those other plans, variables are subject to a 10% penalty if you withdraw your money from them before you reach 59½ years of age. And even though you may make a lot of capital gains on the mutual funds inside the annuities, you still have to pay generally higher ordinary income tax on those gains when you start drawing them down.

What's Inside the Package

When you buy a variable annuity, you get to invest in one or more portfolios called **subaccounts.** There are typically from three to a dozen or more such subaccounts to choose from, just as if you were selecting from a family of funds. In fact, some of the largest fund families—Fidelity, Janus, T. Rowe Price, and Vanguard—offer variable annuities. For instance, you are likely to encounter a growth stock fund, a total-return fund, and one or more bond funds. You may even get to choose an international fund, an asset-allocation fund, a stock index fund, and a fund that invests in only one market sector, such as utilities.

If you're wondering why such a product is called an annuity, here's the reason. When you retire, you can take the money you have accumulated and receive it as a lump sum or as an annuity, which gives you a monthly check for a specified number of years or for the rest of your life. The insurance component is usually a death benefit that guarantees your beneficiaries at least the principal you originally put in the annuity if you should die.

Watch Those Fees

Those sneaky charges have always been the principal stumbling block with annuities, no matter what kind.

(So you don't get confused when an annuity salesperson starts pitching you, understand that most variable annuities are a subspecies of the **deferred annuity,** where the payoff is later on. The other kind, the **immediate annuity,** pays you right away; if you like you can choose to turn your variable into an immediate annuity, dispensing a stream of monthly checks after you retire. The other divide to remember is between variable, whose returns fluctuate because they are invested in portfolios of stocks and bonds that are regularly bought and sold, just as with standard mutual funds; and **fixed,** annuities whose portfolios are full of fixed-income investments and whose returns are set. Consequently if you choose an annuitized payout in exchange for your variable annuity account when you retire, you would likely wind up with a fixed immediate annuity.)

Most annuities have surrender charges, which are similar to the back-end loads that are attached to some mutual funds. But while these loads may be two or three percentage points, surrender charges typically run somewhere from 6% to 9% during the first year you hold your annuity; then they decline by about a percentage point each year until they disappear.

Insurance charges averaging around 1.4% a year are appended to variable annuities. Insurance companies defend this fee on the grounds that it covers the cost of providing an insurance benefit, but as often as not half or more of the insurance charge goes instead to sales commissions, other marketing costs, or just profit.

Then there's the **management fee,** which can run from .75% to more than 1%. This compares to the management fees you will find on all mutual funds. When you add these two fees together, however, total annual charges can exceed 2%, which, as we discussed in Chapter 7, would be considered semioutrageous in a mutual fund.

With these realities in mind, here are the essential tips to bring with you when and if you decide to shop for a variable annuity:

• **Comparison shop at least four or five annuities.**
Competition has become superhot among the insurance companies, mutual funds, and securities firms selling variables—
so much so that variable annuities alone are expected to be a
$100 billion business by the end of 1996. As a result, you'll
find a more competitive range of fees and surrender charges
than were available even a year or two ago. But choosing a
variable annuity is a complicated business, and you should
buy one with the firm intention of holding it for a decade or
longer. So if you don't want to take on the responsibility of
finding the companies that market annuities, sending away
for information on their variable annuity accounts, and deciding for yourself, you may want to consult a fee-only financial
planner (see Chapter 9) in your community who (for an
hourly fee) should be competent to help you make the choice.

Another approach is to order *Morningstar's Variable Annuity Performance Reports,* which give detailed performance
figures on most variable annuities. (Call 800-876-5005; $15
for a single issue.)

• **Consider a "no-load" annuity.** No-loads are relatively new, and some are offered by the biggest mutual
fund companies. Most have no surrender charges and low
insurance company charges ranging from about .55% to
.9%, as opposed to the more traditional 1.4%. Since an
insurance agent or stockbroker usually guides you through
a standard variable annuity contract, a luxury you don't get
when you buy a no-load, you could use a fee-only planner
to perform the service for you with a selection of no-load
funds. The planner might not only explain, but screen out
less desirable annuities. For instance, the profusion of products calling themselves no-load variable annuities are not
all equal; some, for example, might eliminate the surrender
charge but keep the insurance fee high.

• **Pick an annuity with an investment approach you really like.** If only three or four subaccounts are offered, that may not suit your needs, particularly if you are making a sizable commitment of, say, $50,000 or more. If you want to be broadly diversified, eight or more choices might be more to your liking. On the other hand, if your investing style tends toward one or two types of portfolios—like total return or balanced, for example—you should look for annuities with subaccounts that have exemplary performance records in those particular classes of subaccounts. You can even trade off variety for performance—that is, go for an annuity that has only three or four subaccounts if they are the ones you really want to invest in and they have brought in excellent returns.

• **Keep your eye on performance.** Sometimes it's hard to do, given the complexity of these products and the high-powered marketing that is put behind them. Gimmicks are showing up more often, and salespeople make them sound better than they are. For instance, you may be offered a step-up feature that resets the death benefit (after the surrender charge expires) to the annuity's current market value or to the amount you paid in, whichever is higher. This feature is fine if it's present in addition to good performance, but it should never be a main reason for buying. Before putting your money into any subaccount, it's best to look at its performance over three years. Don't settle for one-year records: that's not enough time to gauge the quality of management. This way you'll also filter out all those flashes in the pan that turn up at the top of performance rankings one year and then sink into the depths thereafter.

• **Beware the clones.** These are the subaccounts that are related to well-known mutual funds. Even if the subaccount has the same name and manager as the famous fund, the returns can be quite different. This is sometimes the case because the manager may tend to take a somewhat less aggressive approach with the annuity than with the fund. Again, performance tells the tale.

• **See if you can get the same funds cheaper.** Don't be surprised if you find some famous mutual fund family names being offered by several different annuities. Morningstar's annuity reports identify subaccounts offered by more than one annuity. If you are interested in one of them, compare the insurance charges, which may vary significantly. If you can get the same investment at a lower overall cost, that immediately increases your gain and brings you that much closer to your early retirement.

CHAPTER 15

How to Keep from Outliving Your Money

Throughout history longevity was so rare that it was viewed as a gift, a joy to celebrate, a wonder. No longer. Living to a vintage age is becoming a bit . . . well, common. Octogenarians get no respect for their wisdom or advanced years. And why should they when there are flocks of nonagenarians capering about, acting as if they were 60-year-old kids?

Just take a look at the statistics: The number of people aged 100 or over has doubled every decade since 1950. This is a direct result of the constantly shrinking mortality rates among men and women in their eighties and nineties. In fact, the over-85s have lately been the fastest-growing age group in the United States. What's more, thanks to the splendors of modern medicine, to be old is no longer necessarily to be infirm. The legendary Broadway director George Abbott, who died recently at 107, worked on the revival of his 1950s hit *Damn Yankees* when he was 106. In the coming decades, many more George Abbotts will be turning up, dancing their way past their centenaries. In fact, demographers are projecting that more than a million baby boomers will make it past 100.

That could be a curse. As was discussed at the beginning of this book, a tremendous and totally new responsibility has descended on the shoulders of Americans: to finance a very, very long retirement. But what if it turns out that as hard as you try during your working years, you enter retirement without enough to carry you through the rest of your life? What if you are beaten down by all those enemies of saving and investing we cataloged for you: too many debts—from home mortgages to college bills—to be able to save enough; serious investing losses you couldn't make up in time; too conservative investing habits that didn't allow you to build up enough assets in time; no traditional pension; or, worst of all, a well-paying career cut off too early by corporate downsizing? How can you make up any shortfall without the constantly growing income that Americans learned to expect until the infamous cutbacks that began in the 1980s?

The happy fact is that your ability to make your finances stretch and even grow does not end at retirement. If it did, hope would disappear for those millions of middle-class Americans who just aren't going to save enough by the time they retire to finance a long and carefree later life. In this chapter you'll be introduced to the tools you'll need to cope with this terrifying prospect.

But first, two more core lessons to take to heart:

1. No matter how many years you have before retirement, take this chapter as a timely reminder that the more you do now to save and invest, the fewer prob-

lems you will have trying to make up for a shortfall later on.

2. If you face a shortfall and need the help offered in this chapter, emblazon one word in your memory; write it out 500 times or etch it on your forearm if you think that's what is needed to remember it. It is your new prime enemy, replacing most of the ones you faced during your working life. Its name: *inflation*.

Now get started.

You will need to find out as precisely as possible how large a shortfall you face. If you completed the worksheet called "How Much You Must Save" on page 38, you should have a lock on that information. The worksheet assumes that you will live 10 years beyond today's 17-year life expectancy for a 65-year-old. This added decade is crucial because mere life expectancy is an average number, so that half of the 65-year-olds are destined to live beyond their actuarial expectancy age of 82.

To be safe, more and more financial planners are adding a *minimum* of 10 years to life expectancy for purposes of computing how much money their clients will need for the rest of their lives. Some planners add 15 years, and lately some have simply been assuming that their clients will live to be 100. This is being supersafe, but it's also very expensive, as you'll see if you or your planner ever runs the numbers.

The worksheet also assumes that your retirement fund will grow at a rate of 8% a year, the historical average for a conservative mix of stocks and bonds; and that inflation will run at 5% a year. That too is a conservative estimate because it represents the average for the past 30 years. Many financial planners today use a 4% inflation assumption, which is reasonable since the rate has held closer to 3%

lately and is being watched by a vigilant Federal Reserve. But using 5% gives you an extra layer of protection against your retirement enemy number one.

If you haven't completed the worksheet, now is the time to go back and do so. It is the foundation stone not only of your pre-retirement accumulation, but also of your post-retirement spending. Without knowing how much you'll need, how are you going to figure out at what rate you can spend your nest egg? How are you going to figure in the all-important inflation factor? How will you know how to reallocate your investment portfolio for your later years (how much growth, how much income)? How will you know whether you will need to work at least part-time for a few years? And how will you know whether that irresistible impulse that comes over so many retirees to give generously to their children and grandchildren is a wise estate-planning move (getting assets out of your estate while you're alive) or a foolish and ultimately destructive gesture (ending up with your moving in with the kids after you go broke)?

Here, then, are the best strategies you can use to make up whatever shortfall you find when you complete the worksheet.

Never stop investing for growth. When someone figures out how to vanquish inflation once and for all, you can ignore this commandment. Until then, you should consider it the most indispensable of all rules for post-retirement investing, because it is your best weapon against inflation. Trouble is that it contradicts a strong tradition that says retirees need safety above all and for that reason must keep everything in income investments such as bonds, certificates of deposit, or other cashlike instruments. So it's still common to see people cash out of stocks and stock mutual funds when they retire. That's a major error if you hope to keep up with inflation.

Here is the proof in a nutshell: Studies of various classes of investment agree that only stocks return enough to beat inflation over time. One of the most authoritative is the often quoted study by Ibbotson Associates, the Chicago investment research firm, which tracked investment performance since 1926. The results: Cash has returned 3.7% a year, long-term Treasury bonds 4.7% and stocks 10.2%. With inflation historically running at a 5% rate, as mentioned, the case for equities is irrefutable.

Now the tough question: How much of your money should you be allocating to stocks after you retire? The simplest answer is to rely on a widely used and somewhat conservative rule of thumb: The percentage of your portfolio in stocks or stock mutual funds should be equal to 100% minus your age. So if you are 60, you should put about 40% of your portfolio into stocks or stock funds.

Like all rules of thumb, however, this one somewhat oversimplifies the solution to a problem that is both financial and emotional. In other words, what if putting 40% into stocks at 60, 30% at 70, and so on doesn't do the trick (the financial problem)? And what if putting even that much of your worldly worth into the volatile stock market gives you insomnia, stomach cramps, or worse?

The way to address the financial hangup is to have a competent financial planner do an analysis of your assets and income needs for the rest of your life. The planner can play around with different assumptions and tell you how much you would need to put into stocks so that you never run out of money even if you live 10 or 15 years beyond your life expectancy. The planner can adjust your life span, inflation, rates of return, income, and other factors so you can see how any change affects the outcome. You may find, for instance, that you need to keep only 20% of your portfolio in equities to make your money last. Or it may happen that you need to keep 80% in the stock market. Then what?

That brings us to the emotional issue. Many people, particularly older folks, are simply not comfortable with huge exposure to the stock market. In 1994, for instance, some major growth stock funds dropped 25% or more. Emerging market funds took an even worse beating. Only you can tell how much risk you can stand. But even if you are a daredevil, no prudent adviser would recommend that you put more than, say, 75% of your portfolio into equities after 60. Just as you saw in Chapter 6 how asset allocation becomes slightly more conservative as you move each step from your twenties to your fifties, likewise it continues in this direction as you move from your sixties to your ninties. Exactly what the configuration should be is up to you and your adviser. A consensus among the experts we consulted: Unless you are very rich and have no heirs to think about, don't ever be without some of your money in equities. And hew closer to that rule of thumb as you age. So by the time you're 80, it really is a good idea to limit your exposure to stocks to 20% of your money.

One more important point. Let's say that to make your money last you would have to put more of it into stocks than you feel comfortable with. Then what? That's when you stop, think hard and long about just how much you really, really want to put into equities, and commit not a penny more than that. Of course, you'll still be coming up with a shortfall in your lifetime accounts. But fear not. There are seven more strategies to consider.

Spend down your principal with utmost control. Surprised? Many people are. Without any serious analysis of their prospects, they just assume that investment returns alone will carry them through a long retirement. That $1 million nest egg, more money than most people ever dreamed of amassing in a lifetime, couldn't possibly be dented over time, so of course they'll be able to pass on the principal *intact* to their heirs. The truth? In general, Social Security, a fixed pension, and the return on a modest investment portfolio won't be enough. Most middle-class retirees will have to start drawing down their principal sometime and ought to expect to nibble away at most of it if they live well into their nineties. If you are still surprised, you haven't yet absorbed the lesson of inflation. Take a couple who retire when both are 65 and who have calculated they will need $37,000 a year to live on as they start their new post-job life. By the time they reach 80, with an inflation rate of only 4%, they will require $66,635 a year to live. At 90 the annual figure jumps to $98,636; by 95 it's a lumbering $120,006.

So you'll need to be extra careful to make sure you do not spend too much too soon—a particular danger in the early phase of retirement, when people travel extensively and otherwise indulge themselves. A good guideline: Do not draw off more than 5% of your principal during the first five years of retirement. Any more should ring alarm bells because too much principal eroded early leaves that much less to grow and earn in later years.

In addition, should the stock market take a sharp dive during that time, you may find yourself selling stocks or mutual funds while they are down, which further eats away at principal. Here's another rule of thumb that is especially easy to remember: Don't draw down any more than 6% a year during your sixties, 7% in your seventies, and 8% to 12% in your eighties. Why the spread for octogenarians? Because at that point you're no longer facing down 30 years of retirement and may not require so much principal to grow and compound.

Take those IRA distributions very, very carefully. Now we enter Internal Revenue Service territory, so expect enormous complications for little or no logical reason. But just as with tax preparation, your attention to details here can be amply rewarded. In this case the payoff is being able to make your tax-deferred retirement account stretch and grow to the max.

All retirees who take charge of their 401(k) or other retirement account and subsequently roll it over into an IRA will get a jolt at 70½: you *must* start taking distributions then. If you fail to start withdrawing a minimum each year, you face a draconian penalty: a 50% tax on the amount you should have taken out but didn't.

There are two ways of taking your withdrawals: **recalculation**, where you refigure the amount withdrawn each year based on your changing life expectancy; and **term certain,** where a set schedule is established from the outset. What you must now do is choose the alternative that keeps your minimum annual withdrawals as low as possible. Under law, you can increase the amount any time you like. But by keeping as much as you can in the tax-deferred IRA, you have that much more growing tax-free, especially if you have investments outside your IRA account that you can draw down first. So deciding between the two choices can powerfully affect the continued buildup of your nest egg, as you will see in a moment.

Let's start with recalculation. This is the better route for a couple both of whom are lucky enough to live long lives. The reason: Life expectancy drops less than a full year every year they recalculate. With term certain, by contrast, life expectancy drops a full year every year. So in a few years the couple who go the recalculation route will find themselves withdrawing significantly less than had they gone the term-certain way. *But* should the IRA holder's spouse die early, the minimum usually shoots up, forcing the survivor to take out more than is needed. This problem, curiously enough, does not arise when it is the IRA owner who dies. Then the spouse can simply roll over the contents of the IRA into a "virgin" IRA, naming a child or grandchild as beneficiary. Since the combined age of the spouse and the beneficiary is lower than that of the couple, the minimum drops sharply.

Some experts advise that the uncertainty of the recalculation method generally makes it not worth the trouble. They opt for term certain. Say, for instance, your life expectancy at 70½, as dictated by IRS tables, is 20 years. Then your first year you would have to withdraw one-twentieth of your IRA's value, the second year one-nineteenth, the third year one-eighteenth, and so on. Simple. Of course, some retirees complicate even this scenario when one spouse chooses recalculation and the other term certain—a move fully approved by the IRS. But be warned, you would probably have to find a CPA or some other math whiz to figure out your withdrawals for you.

Here is just one example of how the search for lowering minimums can pay off:

An IRA holder is just turning 70½, his wife is 67, and his account is valued at $300,000. Their combined life expectancy, says the IRS, is 22 years. If they choose the easy way, term certain, they would have to withdraw one twenty-second of the value of the IRA ($13,636) the first year, one twenty-first ($14,636) the second year, one-twentieth ($15,712) the third year, and so on. The IRA would run out at the end of the twenty-first year, assuming 4% annual inflation and an earnings rate of 7% a year. The IRA holder decides instead, with his wife's assent, to designate one of their children or even one of their grandchildren as beneficiary.

This must be done by April 1 of the calendar year in which his seventieth birthday falls. The IRS, for purposes of computing life expectancy, allows a beneficiary to be listed as no more than 10 years younger than the IRA holder. So in this example, the combined expectancy climbs to 26.2 years from 22 years for the first year, with a minimum withdrawal of $11,450 instead of $13,636. The minimum for the second year would be slightly more than 1/25 and the minimum withdrawal $12,235 instead of $14,636, and so on. And here's the real payoff: At the end of the 22 years, the IRA would have a balance of $354,404 instead of having run out completely the year earlier.

If such a strategy appeals to you, please be guided by this blanket warning: Tax lawyers and CPAs who are well versed in the intricacies of IRA distributions are few. And be assured you will need such a pro to pull off one of the more complex distribution schemes. So ask around, consult your local bar association or state CPA society, and stay fully awake through any sessions with the pro you pick, asking as many questions as you can think of. It will be worth the trouble. You might also want to pick up a copy of *J. K. Lasser's How to Pay Less Tax on Your Retirement Savings* (Simon & Schuster), by attorney and CPA Seymour Goldberg.

Take out a reverse mortgage. This is an increasingly popular way to start what amounts to a new pension, with checks coming in every month for the rest of your life. The reverse mortgage is simply a loan secured by your house, which usually must be mortgage-free before you can sign on. The size of your checks will depend on your age, prevailing interest rates, and, of course, your home's market value. The older you are and the more valuable your house is, the higher the checks will be.

The most attractive quality of reverse mortgages is that repayment can be put off until after you vacate the house or die. As we said, it's like a pension: if you die soon after it starts, the bank gets your house for almost nothing—just as your employer gets away with paying out a pittance in pension checks. But if you live well into your nineties, you get to be the big winner. For example, a 70-year-old couple with a $200,000 home might expect to collect about $700 a month.

If you recall reading some unflattering stories over recent years about lenders who were less than forthcoming about the terms of reverse mortgages, you will be pleased to learn that the Federal Reserve Board has come to the rescue of put-upon retirees trying to make ends meet with one of these loans. New Fed rules provide that lenders must make detailed cost disclosures so that consumers can easily compare one reverse mortgage with another. One factor to watch closely: closing costs, which can run to $3,000 or more for a $250,000 house. You can start comparison shopping by calling the Federal Housing Administration at 800-732-6643 and asking for the names of lenders in your area that offer reverse mortgages.

Spend less. This is often far easier for retirees to do than younger folk who are caught between a gargantuan home and college bills on the one hand and minuscule salary raises on the other. Remember that traditional rule of thumb we introduced in Chapter 4—that you will need about 80% of your pre-retirement income? You may also recall that we added a cautionary comment: that most of the best retirement planners we have talked to over the years agree that this is just a general guideline and that the real figure can range anywhere from 50% to 120% or more of your pre-retirement pay.

Particularly in those early retirement years, you may be able to cut back on what are often lavish travel and entertainment expenses. So let's say you have an inkling that you're not quite on top of your overall expenditures. If so, you would be no different from most people. To find out the truth, itemize your checkbook for the past 12 months. List in separate columns your spending on food, housing, travel, transportation, clothing, gifts to relatives, gifts to charities, and so forth. When you know where the money is going, you will be able to determine where you might cut back.

When you've gone through this exercise, you may discover that there aren't enough savings available here to cover your overall shortfall, even after you have nudged more of your portfolio into stocks, dipped judiciously into your principal, adjusted your IRA distributions, and maybe even taken out a reverse mortgage. Then what? Well, then it's time to . . .

Think hard about going back to work. You won't be alone. Indeed, why do a third of retirees hold down some kind of job? It seems obvious that with something like three decades of freedom to look forward to, many just want to keep busy. On the financial side, working part-time even for the first few years of retirement can give a sizable boost to your savings by letting more of your investments grow and compound undisturbed.

But with employers everywhere shrinking their staffs and herding their older employees into early retirement, won't it be fruitless for a sexagenarian to go job hunting? Not really, because it's full-time employees and their expensive benefits that employers want to lose. Highly experienced part-time or temporary workers? Consultants who work freelance or under contract? Come right in. That is part of the reason why temp agencies are booming.

Manpower Inc., the employment-services giant, saw its number of U.S. temps jump 38% between 1990 and 1992—to 750,000 people. And while temping has traditionally been thought of as limited to clerical and service personnel, that is no longer the case. Temping has increasingly been drawing professionals, including doctors and accountants, many of them attracted by the flexible hours. What's more, many laid-off professionals and middle managers who were unable to find new jobs (the unintentionally early retired) have discovered brisk demand for outside consultants—and temps—among downsized companies. You can get a free catalog of books on management consulting by calling Consultants News at 800-531-0007. To dip your toe into the temp waters, start with your local Yellow Pages by looking under "Employment Contractors—Temporary Help."

But before you make any of the above moves, if you are 62 or over, you'll have to check out Uncle Sam to see how far his hand might be lodged in your pocket. Put very simply, federal tax policy treats retirees differently from younger taxpayers—"differently" here being defined as "more harshly." It does this primarily by taking huge bites out of the Social Security checks of retirees who work. For instance, Social Security benefits for those aged 62 to 64 are reduced by $1 for every $2 earned above $8,160. For those aged 65 to 69, $1 is taken away for every $3 earned above $11,280. Those getting top benefits lose it all after earnings exceed $54,444. Because of these penalties, some workers aged 62 to 64 pay a marginal tax rate that can run as high as 104%. That means older workers can wind up paying as much as $1.04 in federal income tax when they earn an additional dollar of income. The rate for workers aged 65 to 69 can run as high as 89%.

The feds get at you another way too—by taxing your Social Security check. When what's called your "provisional income" (your adjusted gross income plus your tax-exempt income plus half your Social Security benefit) tops $25,000 for an individual and $32,000 for a married couple filing jointly, 50% of your Social Security benefit is subject to federal income tax. When you make more than $34,000 as a single or $44,000 as a couple, 85% of your benefit is taxable.

So what's to be done about this taxing obstacle? First of all, when you become eligible for Social Security (at 62 or when you retire, if it's later), try to determine whether you want to or need to work after retirement. Estimate how much you would be earning and figure out how much the penalty and the higher tax bracket would hurt. You'll then be able to see if working is worth it. If so, consider putting off the date you start taking your Social Security benefits. If you start at 62, you receive 20% *less* than at 65. And if you wait till 70, you get 22.5% *more* than at 65. Finally, from 70 on you receive your enhanced benefit no matter how much you earn.

Get your medical costs under control. A catastrophic or debilitating illness requiring an older person to enter a nursing home could wreck even the best-laid plans for financing retirement. The issue here is whether and when you will need to take out a long-term care policy. It is expensive, running from $500 to $1,000 or so when you are 50 up to as much as $7,200 a year by age 79. There is no need to address this issue before 50 and probably no need to actually buy a policy before your sixties. Just recall that you projected your medical and dental costs on the worksheet on page 35. If you made a provision for long-term insurance there, you are covered. If not, consider reviewing Chapter 8 and refiguring the worksheet.

Don't give away money you'll need for yourself. This sounds like a silly thing to do. But talk to any experienced retirement planner and you'll hear tales that could recurl your hair. They're mostly about retirees more generous than wise who think it would be just wonderful to give their kids fat down payments for their first homes or to set up accounts to finance college for their grandchildren. Some even think it's smart financially: why not make tax-free gifts now so the money won't be subject to estate taxes after they die?

Problem is that most of these kind-hearted folks will need the money for their long careers as retirees. Here's the one time you can afford to be generous with your stash: if a careful analysis by you or a competent expert identifies a significant chunk of assets that you can count on leaving behind. And only then. So if you're worried about your heirs' great expectations, consider two thoughts: First, studies persistently show that most grown children feel their parents should spend their money on themselves and are genuinely relieved at the thought that they won't have to support the old folks later on. Second, the traditional and most revered intergenerational legacy is spiritual, not financial. So try to see the guidance, values, and simple love you bestow on your offspring and their offspring as your true legacy. Any worldly asset you leave behind cannot compare.

CHAPTER 16

Five Years to Go: 10 Things to Do

The age you have always wanted to retire is, unbelievably, only five years away. No matter how carefully you have been planning your retirement finances through the years, you should stop now and review some of the factors that will make or break that dream. Five years isn't much time if you're just beginning to save. But it is just about right for a close look followed by a careful repositioning of your finances. That way there will be no hair-raising surprises during the months leading up to your retirement date. (Your failsafe mechanism: Chapter 17, coming up next, which offers a last-minute checklist.) Take the following 10 points to heart and you won't become a pre-retirement head case.

1. Refigure How Much You'll Need.

This is point number one for a very good reason. Just as completing the worksheet in Chapter 4 was an absolute, no-question-about-it necessity, going back and redoing that worksheet is now just as critical. This exercise will tell you just how wide you are of the mark. What if it turns out after recompleting the worksheet that you are seriously short of the total capital you will need to accumulate before you retire? Then the very next move you make is to . . .

2. Reconcile Your Plan with Reality.

If your shortfall is major, and you are sure you have been following a plan religiously, you should first find out what went wrong with your plan. Did your income fail to keep up with expectations? Did your choice of mutual funds underperform? While it is a little late to be finding out such things, they happen. More likely, though, you will find yourself short by a noncatastrophic amount that you might even be able to make up over the next five years. There are several routes you can take, singly or in combination:

First, increase your savings. Can you turn around and save like mad for five years? If so, do it. If you haven't been saving all your raises and bonuses, start there. If you are in the neighborhood of 50, be aware that you are at a dangerous age as a consumer. You're at your earning peak, and the two central spending drains of your life—the house and the kids—are at last off your back. So bit by bit and oh so imperceptibly, you and your spouse have begun treating yourselves to better (and longer) vacations, a nicer wardrobe, a jazzier car (or two), and a couple of mellow restaurant dinners a week. You know where the fat is. Tell yourself it's only for five years, and cut, cut, cut. And invest it all.

Second, put off your retirement date. As mentioned earlier, accruals in your company benefits often accelerate as you get closer to retirement. This is particularly true with old-fashioned defined-benefit pensions. Also, your 401(k) continues to grow, spurred by your employer's contributions and profit sharing. Do a back-of-the-envelope calculation to see roughly how much each year of work adds to your nest egg and then decide whether it is worth it to hang in there for a year or two more.

Third, invest more aggressively. This of course means increasing your risk close to retirement. This is not always the right thing to do, and if done without care, it could be a major mistake. It would be very easy in today's volatile markets, for instance, to move money to riskier investments when they are relatively expensive and then have to sell them when they are down. But sometimes taking on extra risk could be the right thing to do, particularly if you haven't followed the asset allocation set out in Chapter 6 and your portfolio is too conservative in the first place. Among the signs: less than half of your investments are in stocks or stock mutual funds; your stock funds are all low-risk equity-income types and you are shy on growth and aggressive growth funds; more than a quarter or so of your money is in cash-equivalent funds like those that hold guaranteed investment certificates (GICs). If you're thinking of getting more aggressive, you may want to do it with professional help.

3. Consider Hiring a Pro.

You may have gotten this far on your own, and that may be fine. If you know that your savings and investments are keeping pace with the timetable you set up for yourself, no crisis looms on the horizon, and you have been a careful student of your personal finances all through the years, there may be no need to think about getting professional help.

On the other hand, if you are falling behind in your nest egg accumulation, your investment picks are not performing well, or you have other questions you don't feel competent to handle yourself, it may be time to look for a *really good* financial planner. If you wonder why the emphasis is on the *really good*, a quick review of Chapter 9, "Getting the Right Kind of Help," will refresh your memory.

A fee-only planner who comes highly recommended is usually your best bet, particularly at a time when you have a considerable portfolio of investments. A commission planner may be far too tempted simply to dump those investments in favor of ones that will bring him or her commissions. And the itch to sell you financial products you don't need, like costly life insurance, annuities, or long-term-care insurance, might be equally irresistible.

When you find a planner you like, make sure you are completely comfortable with—and totally understand—every move he or she recommends. For example, if the planner wants you to pay, say, $2,000 for a full financial plan, make him or her explain what benefit someone five years from retirement would get from it. (Little, unless it's a post-retirement plan, and now might be a bit soon for that.)

4. Start Paying off All Your Personal Debt.

It is generally a healthy idea to enter retirement debt-free. After all, you will almost certainly be living on a smaller income than your present one, and you will want to leave as much as you can to grow in your investment portfolio instead of using it for expenses. The only exception to this rule has to do with your house. If, for instance, you are still carrying a substantial mortgage, and current mortgage rates are two points or so below the rate you are carrying, you may want to look into refinancing. If you wait until after you retire, banks may be less eager to do business with you when you are no longer receiving a full salary. Also check out the cost of shortening the term of the mortgage, which will save you lots of interest dollars in the long run. And consider a fixed instead of an adjustable mortgage. As a general rule, it is prudent to keep your post-retirement expenses fixed wherever possible.

5. Focus Harder on Where You Will Live.

Granted, there's a huge emotional element in this decision. Perhaps that's why most retirees just stay put in the home they've lived in for many years. But more and more people are investigating the adventuresome option of retiring in a different part of the country (Chapter 11) or of the world (Chapter 12). The reason we bring this up now is that there is also a huge financial element involved. So the earlier you decide on where and when, the better. Here are some leading considerations:

If you stay put. Will you be able to pay off your mortgage by the time you retire? If not, how long will you have to deal with this major expense? Have you considered the possibility of moving to a smaller place in your town or neighborhood? That way you would be staying put in your community but possibly sharply reducing your carrying charges, property taxes, and energy bills, while at the same time pocketing the difference between what you got for your old larger house and what you pay for the new one.

If you trade down. Typically, those people who retire and move south—to Florida, for instance—wind up with a windfall like the one we just described: the difference between what their new house costs and what they got for their old one.

If this is your plan, even though it's five years early, you should estimate how much that wad will amount to and figure it into your post-retirement finances. It could make a big difference and even inspire you to retire earlier than you thought you could. Another key point, stated in Chapter 11 but repeated here for emphasis: If you are planning to move to a distant place, it is essential to spend as much time there in as many seasons of the year as you can before you make a final decision. Five years before R Day is not too soon to start these pilgrimages.

If you buy a second home. This is the choice of many retirees who want to hold on to the homestead and have a retreat in the sun or up at the lake. While this is of course the most expensive way to go, many retirees do it with an eye to eventually giving up the homestead and making the vacation house their full-time retirement home.

Whatever your decision, it will involve considerable variations in costs. You should work these out, at least in the rough, so you will know you can afford the expenses. Doing the math may also cause you to alter your plans. If so, you shouldn't wait until you're on the brink of retirement before finding out the financial facts.

6. Take a Whole New Look at Your Asset Allocation.

Way back in Chapter 6, you learned that an amazing 92% of an investor's returns come from the correct combination of assets. You also read that study after study confirmed that investors are generally too conservative with their money, with the result that their portfolios don't grow as fast as they otherwise would. Even in this chapter you were invited—very carefully—to consider getting more aggressive in your investments if you found yourself falling behind in your capital accumulation plan. Now, after all that, you're being asked to take a completely fresh, objective look at your asset allocation. What gives? Doesn't anybody trust you? Well, yes and no. This matter transcends trust. It is just that important. What you should do is simple:

First, put together all of your investments, those inside your 401(k) or other tax-deferred plan, any other company savings plan, annuities, Keoghs, IRAs, and any bank and brokerage accounts you have. Leave nothing out. When you allocate, you have to do it with all of your assets.

Second, go back to your basic allocations (Chapter 6 again) for each age and see how your current allocation veers from your original plan.

Third, rejigger by reducing and adding to the amounts you have in various mutual funds until your overall portfolio is back in line with your allocation model.

That's all. Sounds almost too simple, but you might be amazed at how far a set of investments can drift off its allocated course.

Oh, one more thing. Don't forget to do this every year from now on.

7. Check Your Life Insurance.

If you're like most people, you have never developed the habit of pulling your life insurance policies out of the drawer and evaluating them every few years. Chances are the only time you pay close attention to them is when an insurance salesman comes calling, and you soon find yourself the owner of a brand new policy.

The point here is that your greatest need for life insurance may have passed, yet you may be paying high premiums that are being at least partly wasted. So gather up your policies. Look over your responsibilities. Are your offspring grown and out of the house? Are you not the sole breadwinner? If you were to die, would your spouse and other dependents be financially secure *without* the proceeds of your insurance? If so, you are overinsured.

You may still want to carry some coverage, but should it be in cheaper term life or in more expensive whole life, with its cash buildup? Do you know whether your employer will continue to insure you after you retire? If you've found a reliable fee-only financial planner, he or she can help you sort out your life insurance questions. Alternatively, you can call an outfit like the Life Insurance Advisers Association (800-521-4578). For a fee, an adviser will assess your coverage and costs for you.

8. Make Realistic Plans about Postwork Work.

You can look on this as one of your escape valves. By working out an honest assessment of your employment possibilities after retirement, you accomplish two wonderfully confidence-building things. First, you identify another income source should you need it. Second, you create a potential outlet if you find that you don't want to live with retirement without some work. You might want to review our discussion of this topic in Chapter 15, "How to Keep from Outliving Your Money."

Note the emphasis on realistic plans. Is there anyone who doesn't spend his or her working life daydreaming about an ideal way of earning a living, perhaps something like running a great little restaurant or bed-and-breakfast or country hotel or bookstore antique shop? These enterprises are realistic for only a few people who have an entrepreneur's spirit and endless amounts of energy to expend on the long hours and, often, hard work. And everywhere you turn today, there is so much competition in small business that serenity is one thing you aren't likely to achieve by going out on your own.

Again realistically, as Chapter 15 points out, opportunities for part-time or even full-time work for older people are growing. And that trend is sure to continue and expand just because it will be so hard for most people to retire and finance 30 years of retirement without continuing to work. In fact, some experts believe that the era of total retirement at 55 or 60 or 65 is merely a blip in history, one that is already fading.

So your first homework assignment on the subject of working after retirement is to make a list of the kinds of work you're both good at and enjoy. Then start assessing— using the resources mentioned in Chapter 15—the demand out there for what you have to supply. Keep on probing from time to time over the next four years. By your last pre-retirement year, you ought to have a short list of job prospects ready to pursue if and when you want to do so.

9. Visit Your Benefits People.

It's a mistake to wait until near the very end to talk to your company's benefits department, because there are almost certainly topics you don't know enough about that will substantially affect your retirement finances. Like:

Your pension. Now is the time to ask for an assessment of the size of your pension. It's essential that you know these numbers early so you can calculate your retirement finances in a more and more detailed way as you approach the jumping-off point. You'll most likely get an estimate of your annual pension, calculated in several ways: as a single-life annuity, as a 50% joint-and-survivor annuity, as a 100% joint-and-survivor annuity, as a 10-year period-certain annuity, and perhaps a couple of other ways.

The single-life amount will be the highest because it goes to you for the rest of your life. Period. The 10-year certain annuity will probably generate the next highest annual amount because it will be paid out for exactly 10 years, even if you should die earlier. Consequently, a 15-year-certain annuity pays a bit less. The 50% joint-and-survivor annuity comes next: it continues paying—say, your spouse—half what you were getting should you die. A 100% joint-and-survivor, which keeps on paying the whole amount to your survivor, pays out the least from the start. And you will also receive an estimate of the amount of your lump sum if your employer allows you that choice.

Your medical benefits. These are changing more rapidly than ever as employers try to reduce the frightening growth of health care insurance. Find out exactly how much your coverage will cost you after you retire. If you are retiring before 65, you'll have to wait until that age to get Medicare. Will the company help you out? And will it do anything for you after you turn 65, like providing inexpensive Medigap coverage as some generous employers do, or even long-term-care insurance, a small but fast-growing trend among larger employers?

Your life insurance. Some employers maintain your coverage up to 65 even if you retire early. Some have other goodies that could enable you to cut way back on your private coverage.

Your spouse. Now is the time to find out if your employer's post-retirement benefits are a lot better than those of your spouse's employer. You may want to enroll your spouse in your plan before you retire so that he or she will be able to share in those gifts after you both are retired.

Help. Ask what kind of guidance the company will give you as you prepare to retire. For instance, it may sponsor free seminars, held by knowledgeable pros, for you and your spouse. Make sure you sign up.

10. Call Social Security.

You were supposed to do this when you filled out the worksheet in Chapter 4, "The Key: How Much You Will Need." Since now is the right time to review everything, it would be wise to make that call again (800-772-1213) and get a completely up-to-date projection of your Social Security benefit.

CHAPTER 17

Six Months to Go: Nine Things to Do

Glory be, the end is near. But first there are a few things you'll need to act on during the final six months before your last 'night, all. Do each of them carefully and with deliberate speed. The old warning about hasty marriages serves well here, too: Retire in haste, repent at leisure. Thirty years' worth.

1. Re-refigure How Much You'll Need.

In Chapter 16 you were advised to refigure the worksheet in Chapter 4 that shows you how much you need to save each year so you'll have enough for your retirement. Now is the moment in your life when you get to tot up all the saving and investing you've done over the years to see how close you are to what you'll need.

If you carefully followed the advice in Chapter 16, you

won't get any nasty surprises now. But you should at least review the worksheet this one last time because all of the figures you've entered on it—which are just rough estimates when you're decades away from retirement—will be at their firmest now. So you'll get the most credible bottom line now. If by some chance you are wide of the mark, review Chapter 15 for advice on what to do about it. If, for instance, it is too late to put off your retirement, you're saving all you can, and you don't dare get more aggressive in your investing, you may need to look into post-retirement employment.

2. Notify Your Company's Benefits Department.

The folks who process your retirement paperwork—human resources, benefits, personnel or whatever they're called at your company—usually want you to tell them your planned retirement date about six months ahead. While this is convenient for them, it is also helpful for you because you will be going over a number of complicated issues that you will want to think about, then discuss at a second meeting to raise any questions you may have. For instance, the benefits people will be computing the final numbers for your pension and they will be explaining what benefits you will lose, which ones will be cut back, and which ones, if any, will stay in place. The next two points expand on these matters.

3. Rewire Your Benefits.

As indicated in Chapter 16, the principal benefits you'll be looking at are health and life insurance. Since Medicare won't kick in until you're 65, early retirement may mean footing the entire bill for your health care coverage until then. Your benefits people may be able to help you here. Your group life insurance will likely end when you retire or possibly stay in force until you're 65. In either case, you may not need the kind of death-benefit coverage you had to have when you had small children. You may not need any life insurance at all, for that matter. Many retirees have policies solely for use in helping settle their estates. But that's an entirely different matter that must be discussed with your financial planner or an estate lawyer. Your company disability insurance may also have outlived its usefulness, unless you are sure you will need to work to some extent after you retire.

4. Decide: Lump Sum or Annuity.

Remember from Chapter 13: Annuities can't keep up with inflation, but if you manage a lump sum well, you can invest for growth and thereby conquer that rapacious inflation beast. The catch: You have to manage it well, and that's a big responsibility. Well, now comes the moment of truth. You must choose between the two, and your decision will be irrevocable.

A smart, honest, fee-only financial planner can help you make up your mind. He or she will not only assess your strengths and weaknesses as a money manager, but can also analyze the annuity and the lump sum and tell you if one or the other is a better deal. The analysis is complex: don't think about doing it yourself, and don't leave it in the hands of a planner you don't trust.

5. Work out Where Your Stash Will Be Invested.

If you take an annuity, you don't have to worry about this point as far as your pension is concerned. If you take a lump sum, you have to determine the disposition of it *plus* your 401(k) or other tax-favored savings plan. Assuming you roll the money over into an IRA, usually the best deal, you must tell your company where to direct the funds, and it all must be done within 60 days (Chapter 13 again). This will probably mean choosing a mutual fund family or families.

Your financial planner will guide you on this move. If you don't have a planner, you must do your homework during this period. You not only need to become familiar with fund families, you also need to choose which funds within your chosen family you want for your money. Return to Chapter 6 and use the asset allocation outlined for your age. And if you haven't done so already, start reading newspapers and magazines, such as **MONEY**, that feature strong mutual fund coverage.

6. Set up a Home-Equity Line of Credit.

If you've followed the advice in Chapter 16, you will by now have paid off your personal debt, or at least most of it. Even though your credit record may be exemplary, lenders may become a lot less eager to let you borrow once you are retired and your income has shrunk. So just in case an emergency surfaces and you really need to borrow, set up a home-equity line of credit now. You can draw on it any time you want and take out as much as you want without having to go through the standard credit routine. The interest is not only far lower than that on credit cards, but it is also fully deductible. Since making use of this credit line puts your home in hock, use it sparingly. Another reasonable use: to consolidate your debts and reduce their cost.

7. Check out Reverse-Mortgage Deals.

These, as you may recall from Chapter 15, provide you with a way to give yourself a second pension tied to the value of your house. You gradually sell the equity in your home to a bank, getting monthly checks in a kind of reversal of the standard mortgage, which requires you to send the bank a monthly check. As Chapter 15 points out, these can be lifesavers for retirees who see they are running out of money.

Here's another way of looking at the reverse mortgage if you're determined to retire early but find six months ahead of the target date that the numbers just don't add up, that you will need more than you have to finance that 30-year golden phase. You may want to use some of your retirement plan money to open a business; the income from a reverse mortgage could take the place of that cash.

But what of the risk? Is it prudent to gamble with the roof over your aging head? You can avoid that danger by taking out a **tenure reverse mortgage**, which brings you those monthly checks for the rest of your life. The alternative is the **term reverse mortgage**, which runs for a set time, usually no more than 20 years. Then the bank sells the house. The older you are, the more you get in your checks. A single person with a house worth $200,000 might receive around $700 a month at age 70, running up to $1,500 a month at age 85. Generally to qualify for a reverse mortgage one of the spouses must be at least 62 and the mortgage must be paid off. Think you're going to live a very long life? Just contemplate the most renowned reverse-mortgage holder in the world, the French widow who took out the loan in her eighties and at last report was still going strong in her old homestead at a ripe 120.

8. Decide about Social Security.

If you are at least 62 when you retire, you can start receiving your Social Security checks right away. But you should apply for them a few months before they're supposed to start so you won't miss any. Remember, however, that if you do start on Social Security at 62, you will get only 80% of the total benefit for the rest of your life. It's a complicated decision, and one you need to make in the context of your entire financial outlook. For instance, it might be better to jump in at 62 if doing so enables you to leave your retirement money growing undisturbed in your rollover IRA for a longer time.

9. Start Letting Go.

Hallelujah, your rebirth is at hand. Then why aren't you bursting with anticipation, joy, and a warm pity for your poor fellow slaves? If you're like most of the about-to-be-retired, you're a sensitive human being who will not be able just to slam the door on a life of work and skip away. You'll miss a lot of people. Perversely, you'll find you miss a lot about the very routine of your job.

While this is all predictable and natural, it can get out of hand if you let it. Now, during these last six months, is the time to start distancing yourself from the world of your office. You don't have to start finding fault with your boss

175

or your colleagues. Far from it. The trick is to focus your thoughts more and more on what you will be doing after you call it quits. What will the days be like? Have you thought about how you'll structure them? What will your first project be? Your second? You mean you haven't yet started planning the most dreamed-about trip of your life? There's so much to do, so much to think about. There. You're letting go already. It's all right to look back, but not for too long.

INDEX

Abbott, George, 144–45
ADV Form, Part II, 86, 91
*Adventures Abroad: Exploring the
    Travel Retirement Option* (Parker
    and Symons)
Aggressive growth investments, 161
Agressive growth funds, 67–68
Aiken, South Carolina, 112–13
Alabama, 106–7
Albuquerque, New Mexico, 115
Alimony, 52
"Aloneness" concept, *xii*
Alternative medicine, 101
Alzheimer's disease, 101
American Association of Retired
    Persons (AARP), 15, 98
American College, 83
American Institute of Certified
    Public Accountants, 84
American Stock Exchange, 62
Americans
    fixed-income investments and,
        49–50

savings rate, 3
Annuities, 9, 165
    choice of, 127–28
    compared with lump-sum
        distributions, 128–31, 172
    single-life *vs.* joint-and-survivor
        option, 129
    See also Variable annuities
Appalachians, 114
Arizona, 105–6, 111
Arkansas, 113
Asheville, North Carolina, 116
Asian countries, 55
Asset allocation, 49–53, 80
    amount of risk, 67
    and fund families, 69–70
    in 401(k)s, 78–80
    model portfolios, 53–61
    reassessment of, 165
Asset-allocation funds, 77, 139
Association for Investment
    Management and Research,
    84

Asthma, 101
Averaging. *See* Income averaging

Baby boom generation
  healthier retirements, 13
  part-time work after retirement,
    20
  retirement income sources, 22–23
  and Social Security, 22–24
Balanced funds, 68, 77
Bank accounts, 165
Beebower, Gilbert, 49
Beneficiaries, 128
  of IRAs, 152–53
  of Social Security, 28–29
Benefits departments, 168–69, 171
Blue chips, 54–55, 59
  See also Large-cap funds; Large-
    cap stocks
Blue Ridge mountains, 114
Bond funds, 56, 70, 78, 139
  and risk, 67
Bonds, 47, 147
  bull market (1980s), 48
  investments, early 30s, 57
  and mutual funds, 50–51
  returns compared with stocks,
    49–50
Brevard, North Carolina, 114–15
Bridging, 43
Brinson, Gary P., 49
Brokerage accounts, 165
Brokerage wrap accounts, 89–90
Bull markets, 59
  1980s, 48, 64

California, 104–5, 111–12
Cancer, 101
Capital gains, 67
  tax on IRA rollovers, 134
Certificates of deposit (CDs), 10,
    147

CFA (chartered financial analyst),
    83–84
CFP (certified financial planner), 83
Chapel Hill, North Carolina,
    109–10
Charitable gifts and contributions,
    35
Charles Schwab, 70
Charleston, South Carolina, 119
Checking accounts, 5, 165
ChFC (Chartered financial
    consultant), 83
Children and grandchildren, 34,
    138, 152, 158
Clayton, Georgia, 119–20
Clothing expenses, 34
COBRA (Consolidated Omnibus
    Budget Reconciliation Act,
    1986), 98
College education costs, 3–4, 34,
    58, 85
  grandchildren accounts, 158
Colorado, 115
Commission-only financial
    planners, 85
Companies. *See* Company plans;
    Corporations; Downsizing
    companies
Company plans, 22, 36–37, 74–79,
    165
  benefit projections, 37
  and company stock, 78–79
  as part of retirement income, 22
Compound interest, *xi-xii*, 7, 8
  average annual rates of return, 76
  and tax-free IRAs, 52
  See also Interest rates
Computer software, 32, 40
Conflicts-of-interest, 24, 84, 85, 92
Congress, 24, 97, 99–100, 128
  See also Federal government
Consultant News, 156
Consultants, 20, 42, 90, 156
Consumerism, 3–4
Convertible bond funds, 56, 78

Corporate bonds, 78
  rate of return for long-term, 76
Corporations
  benefits departments, 97, 168–71
  early-out offers and bridging, 43
  health care for retirees, 96–100,
    168–69
  See also Company plans;
    Downsizing companies
Cost-of-living adjustments, 23–24,
  127
Costa Rica, 122
CPAs, 84, 152
  See also Tax accountants
Credit cards
  interest on, 173–74
  payments, 5, 7, 34
Currency fluctuations, 55

Damn Yankees, 144
Debt, 163, 173–74
Defense industry, 42
Deferred annuity, 139–40
Defined-benefit pensions. See
    Annuities; Lump-sum
    distributions; Pensions
Dennis, Helen, 15
Developing countries, 68
Diversification, 19, 69
Dividends, 67
Divorce, 29
Doctors, 96, 98, 156
Downsizing companies, 10–11, 20,
  145
  and buyout evaluation, 41–45
Durango, Colorado, 115

Early retirement
  buy-out offers, 42–46
    warning, 43
  college education costs, 34
  health care coverage, 96–99

percentage of Social Security
    benefits, 27, 37
Education (continued after
    retirement), 20, 34
Elderhostel Program, 20
Emerging-markets funds, 55, 68
Employers. See 401(k)s; Pensions
Equitable Life, 22
Equity-income funds, 48, 59, 68, 77
Estate, 128
  taxes, 158
Expenditures, estimates of, 5–6

Fairhope, Alabama, 106–7
Far Eastern countries, 55
Fayetteville, Arkansas, 113
Federal government, 20, 24
  health costs, 95–96
  See also Congress
Federal Housing Administration,
  154
Federal Reserve Board, 154
  telephone number, 59
Fee-and-commission financial
    planners, 84–85
Fee-for-service medicine, 96
Fee-only financial planners, 84, 141
  advice on choosing lump-sum
    distribution or annuity, 172
Fidelity
  fund family, 69–70, 139
  Retirement Planning Thinkware,
    40
Financial analysts, 92
Financial planners, 32, 81, 83–88,
  85, 92
  and ADV Form, Part II, 86
  cautions and questions to ask,
    85–88
  certifications, 83
  commission-only category, 85–86
  expansion of life expectancy, 146
  fee-and-commission category,
    84–85

fee-only category, 84
lump-sum distribution and, 131,
    136
minimum qualifications, 85
recommended savings
    percentages, 4–5
references and record, 87–88
rule of thumb for necessary
    retirement income, 2
selection of, five years before
    retirement, 162
Social Security forecasts, 25
and variable annuities, 141
Five-year averaging, 132–33
Fixed annuities, 140
    See also Annuities
Fixed-income investments, 53, 56,
    57, 77
Americans and, 49–50
and risk, 67
    See also Bond funds; Bonds
Florida, 104, 107–8, 110, 164
Food costs, 33
Foreign exchange fluctuations,
    124–25
403(b)s, 9, 51–52, 74, 76, 137
401(k)s, xii, 7–8, 42, 71, 165
at 70½ years, 151
asset-allocation, 78
borrowing from, 77–78
compared with variable annuities,
    137–38
federal penalty for early
    withdrawal, 77
growth and inflation-protection
    portion of retirement fund,
    129
large contributions, 77
maximum allowable in 1975, 75
monitoring of, 75–78
offered by employer, 74–80
tax savings example, 51–52
France, 124
Fund families, 69–70

GATT treaty provision, 128
Georgia, 119–20
Germany, 124
GICs (guaranteed investment
    contracts), 77
Goldberg, Seymour, 153
Government
employees and downsizing,
    41–45
taxes on benefits and pensions, 33
    See also Federal government;
        State governments
Government bonds
funds, 77
long-term, 76
Graham, Benjamin, 51
Great Smokies, 114
Growth and income funds, 68
Growth funds, xi, 48, 55–56, 59,
    60–61, 67, 77, 79, 139
for inflation protection, xi, 129
overweighted in technology, 69
and risk, 67
Growth stocks, xi
and compound interest, 7
in tax-deferred plans, 75–76

Health care coverage, 42, 95–102,
    171–72
assessment at retirement, 168
insurance costs for individuals,
    43–44
Heirs, 128
and tax-free gifts, 158
    See also Beneficiaries; Children
        and Grandchildren
Hendersonville, North Carolina,
    117
High-yield bond funds, 56, 78
HMOs (health maintenance
    organizations), 96, 100, 101
Hobbies, cost of, 34
Home-equity line of credit, 173–74
Honduras, 122

Housing
  change of location, 163–64
  post-retirement costs, 32
"How to Retire Rich" (Moss
  Adams), 37

Ibbotson Associates, 76, 148
Immediate annuity, 139–40
Income. See Retirement income
Income averaging, 131–34, 135–36
  four requirements for, 132
  taxes and employer contributions,
    132–33
Index funds, 70–71
Individual Retirement Accounts. See
  IRAs; Rollover IRAs
Inflation, xi
  and annuities, 127
  drawing down of principal,
    149–51
  future rate of, 37–38
  and 401(k)s, 129
  and retirement income, 2–4,
    144–58
  as retirement's prime enemy, 146,
    150
  stock returns and, 148
Institute for Investment
  Management Consultants,
    90–91
Insurance, 32
  double caveat: your lump-sum
    distributions, 131
  early retirement and health care,
    43–44
  life and disability, 34
  and Medigap policies, 99
  sales representatives, 81–82,
    92–94, 131
  variable annuities and, 141, 143
  See also Health care coverage; Life
    insurance; Long-term care
    insurance
Interest rates

  on credit cards, 173–74
  and lump-sum distributions, 128,
    130
  See also Compound interest
Intermediate-term bond funds, 56,
  57
International Board of Standards
  and Practices for Certified
  Financial Planners, 83
International stock and bond funds,
  50, 54–55, 67, 70, 77–78, 139
  management fees, 66
  in various portfolios, 53, 57, 58,
    59, 60–61
International stocks, 55, 59
Investment bankers, 92
Investment management
  consultants, 90
Investments, 47–61, 74
  amount of risk, 9–10
  post-retirement, 34–35, 37,
    146–49, 161
  stocks as priority, 49–50
  See also Asset allocation; Financial
    planners; Mutual funds
IRAs, 71, 137–38, 165
  importance of, 74
  investing through, 51
  mandatory withdrawals at 70½
    years, 151–53
  See also Rollover IRAs
Ireland, 122
IRS (Internal Revenue Service)
  mandatory IRA withdrawals,
    151
  publications, 124
  See also Taxes

J. K. Lasser's How to Pay Less on
  Your Retirement Savings
  (Goldberg), 153
Janus fund family, 139
Japan, 124
Job security, 10–11

Joint-and-survivor annuity, 129, 168

"Junk" bonds, 56

Keogh plans, 9, 74, 132, 134, 137–38, 165
tax-savings example, 51–52
Kerrville, Texas, 114

Large-cap funds, 70, 78
management fees, 66
Large-cap stocks
average annual rates of return, 76
in various portfolios, 53–55, 57, 58–61
Las Vegas, Nevada, 108–9, 117
Latin America, 55, 68
Life expectancy, 13, 37, 146
and lump sum distributions, 128
recalculation or term certain withdrawals, 151–53
Life insurance, 171–72
caveat: single-life annuity option with insurance protection for spouse, 129
variable annuity guarantee, 138, 139
when nearing retirement, 34, 166, 169
Life Insurance Advisers Association, 166
Lifestyle Explorations, 124
Load funds, 51, 70
buying of, 64–66
Long-term care insurance, 101, 157–58
Long-term corporate bonds, 76
Lump-sum distributions, 127–31
choice of mutual fund families, 173
compared with annuity, 172
double caveat: financial advice needed, 130–31

and income averaging, 132–34
and interest rate assumptions, 128
interest rate rule of thumb, 130
Lynch, Peter, 68

Magellan Fund, 68
Managed care operations, 96, 98
See also HMOs
Manpower, Inc., 156
Market timing, 71
Married couples
health care coverage cost, 97–98
and IRAs, 8–9, 52
medical and dental costs, 33
spending ranges for, 5–6
Medicare, 96–97, 123
future changes in, 99–100
and politics, 95–96, 99
Medicare Select, 100
Medigap insurance, 99–100
Mexico, 122
peso fluctuations, 68, 125
Midcap funds, 48, 67, 70, 78
management fees, 66
Midcap stocks, 54–55, 59, 61
Middle managers, 156
Minimum-distribution allowance, 134
MONEY magazine, 65, 173
on managing your own financial plan, 82
Money managers, 81, 88–92
avoidance of 3% fee, 89–90
record and performance, 91–92
stockbroker referrals, 90–91
Morningstar Inc., 65
Morningstar's Variable Annuity Performance Reports, 141, 143
Mortgages, 57
payments, 32
refinancing of, 163
Moss Adams accounting firm, 37
Mount Dora, Florida, 107–8
Municipal bond funds, 59–61

Mutual funds, 47
  buy and hold strategy, 63–64, 70
  capital gains distributions, 89
  choosing of, 62–73
  diversification, 48, 69
  getting information on, 72
  international investments and, 50
  investing through, 50–53
  management fees, 66
  optimum number to own, 68–70
  reasons for selling, 73
  and risk, 71
  sales representatives of, 92–94
  subaccounts, 139, 142
  tax-deferred, 137–43
  See also names of types of funds,
    eg. Bond funds; Portfolios;
    Variable annuities
Myrtle Beach, South Carolina,
  116–17

Naples, Florida, 110
National Association of Securities
  Commissioners, 81–82
National Association of Securities
  Dealers (NASD), 87–88
  list of fraudulent financial
    planners, 94
  toll-free telephone number, 93
Nevada, 108–9
New England, 107
New Jersey, 105
New York Stock Exchange, 62
"No-load" annuity, 141
No-load funds, 51, 70
  bonds, 56
  buying of, 65, 66
  explained, 64–66
North Carolina, 109–10, 114–15,
  116, 117–18

Olympic Mountains, 118

Paris, 121, 124–25
Parker, Jane, 122
Part-time work, 19–20, 155–56
Pennsylvania, 105
Pensions, *ix, xii*, 75, 150, 154
  assessment of, 168
  averaging or rollover IRA,
    131–34
  cost-of-living adjustments, 23
  early-retirement offers and, 42–43
  and life expectancy, 2
  lump sum or annuity, 127–31
  taxes on, 33
  vis-a-vis final pre-retirement pay,
    37–38
  See also Company plans
PFS (personal financial specialist),
  84
Portfolios:
  1. twenties to early thirties, 53
  2. early thirties to forties, 57–58
  3. early forties to fifties, 58–60
  4. early fifties to sixties, 60–61
  percentage invested in stocks after
    retirement, 148
  reassessment of, 165
  and subaccounts, 139, 142
Portugal, 122
Pre-retirement income, 2, 31–32
  See also Retirement income
Prescott, Arizona, 105–6
Professionals, 156
  temporary-work after retirement,
    42
Property taxes, 32
"Provisional" income, 26

Quiz (readiness for retirement),
  16–19

Real estate, 3
Recalculation method, 151–53
Recreation expenses, 34

Relatives, support of, 34
Repairs, 32
Residence. *See* Housing
Retailing industry, 42
Retirement
  checklist when five years away,
    159–69
  checklist when six months away,
    170–76
  enforced early, 10–11
  medical and dental costs after,
    33–34, 157
  part-time work, schooling, and
    volunteering, 19–21, 34
  positive or negative reasons for,
    14–15
  putting off of, 161
  readiness test, 14–19
  as third quarter of life, 13
  vacations compared with, 14
  working after, 19–21, 155–57
Retirement abroad, 121–25
  job opportunities, 123
  recommendations, 122
Retirement age
  and early-retirement offers, 44–45
  income averaging of lump-sum
    distributions, 132–34
  and increased longevity, 144–45
  raising of, for Social Security
    beneficiaries, 24
  readiness text, 16–19
  and Social Security benefits, 24,
    26–28
Retirement in America video series
  (Tillman), 120
Retirement income
  amount needed, 2, 30–40,
    145–46, 154–55
  examples of, 2, 7
  drawing down on principal,
    149–51
  growth investments and inflation
    rates, 146–49
  IRA withdrawals, 151–53

reverse mortgages, 153–54
from Social Security, 22–28
Retirement locations
  moving to new, 102–4, 163–64
  seven characteristics of, 105
  top twenty in U.S., 105–20
  See also Retirement abroad
Retirement planners. *See* Financial
  planners
Retirement-planning computer
  software, 39–40
Retirement-planning seminars, 15,
  169
Retirement savings plans. *See*
  403(b)s; 401(k)s; Savings
Returns
  average annual rate, 7, 76
  with tax-deferred savings plans, 8
Reverse mortgages, 153–54, 174–75
"RIFfed" (reduction in force)
  employees, 41–45
Risk, 9–10
  asset-allocation models and, 67
  foreign exchange markets and, 58
  lowering of, 57, 58–60
  and small-cap/international
    stocks, 54–55
Rollover IRAs
  avoidance of taxes, 135–36
  and lump-sum distributions,
    131–36
  Social Security benefit at 62 and,
    175
  tax breaks on, 134
  and taxes, 131
Russell 2000 index, 70, 91
Russell earnings-growth index, 91

St. George, Utah, 117
San Antonio, Texas, 114
Savings, *ix-xii*
  Americans and, 3
  annual goal, 47
  automatic method, 6

commitment to, 6–7
example: amount needed to reach
    $1 million, 7
ideal range for spending
    categories, 5–6
increased, when five years from
    retirement, 160–61
from managed health care plans,
    98
plans, 74–80
post-retirement, 34–39
strategies for, 1–7
See also Tax-deferred savings
    plans
Second homes, 164
Sector funds, 71
Securities and Exchange
    Commission (SEC), 81, 85, 86,
    91
verification of financial planners'
    record, 87–88
Sedona, Arizona, 111
Self-employment, 134
and tax-deferred savings, 9
SEPs, 9, 74
Sequim, Washington, 118
Singer, Brian D., 49
Single-life annuity, 129, 168
Single persons
company's cost for medical
    coverage, 98
and IRAs, 8, 52
spending ranges for, 5–6
Small-business owners, 9
Small-cap funds, 68–69, 70, 77–78
management fees, 66
and risk, 67
Small-cap stocks
average annual rates of return, 76
cuts in, fifties to sixties, 61
and risk, 54–55
trimming of, early thirties, 57
Small stocks and bonds, 50
Smart-aleck funds, 71

Social Security, *ix, xii,* 123, 127,
    150
beginnings (1935), 13
benefit estimates, 36, 38
benefit projections, 25, 36–37,
    169
computer programming of
    benefits, 40
cost-of-living adjustments,
    23–24, 127
and divorced beneficiaries, 29
eligibility, 28–29
future changes and fixes to,
    24–25
and longer life expectancy, 2
maximum benefit (1995), 23
as part of retirement income,
    22–28, 74
retirement age, 24, 26
starting ages and benefit amount,
    26–28, 175
survivor's benefits, 28–29
taxes and work after retirement,
    156–57
taxes on benefits, 24, 26–27, 33
trust fund deficits and cuts, 24
Social Security Administration
    (SSA), 36–37
telephone number, 25
Software, for retirement-planning,
    40
South Carolina, 112–13, 116–17,
    119
Southern states, 105, 106–11,
    112–15, 116–20
Southwest, 105–6, 111, 115, 117
S&P 500. *See* Standard & Poor's
    500 stock index
Special averaging, 131–32
Spousal benefits
from employers, 169
from life insurance policy, 129
from Social Security, 28–29
Standard & Poor's 500 stock index,
    65, 69, 70, 91

State governments, 97
  requirements for financial
    planners, 85
Stock funds
  in asset-allocation portfolio, 78
  and risk, 67
Stock index funds, 139
Stock pickers, 51
Stockbrokers, 10, 81–82, 141
  as financial managers, 92–94
  lump-sum distribution and, 131
  for referrals to money managers,
    90–91
  sale of mutual funds, 62
Stocks, 47, 57
  higher returns and investment
    priority, 49–50
  historical returns, 148
  industrial balance in, 48
  and mutual funds, 50–51
  See also names of stocks and
    funds, eg. Growth funds;
    Large-cap stocks; Value
    stocks
Sunbelt states, 105
Symons, Allene, 122

T. Rowe Price, 69
  fund family, 139
  Retirement Planning Kit, 40
Tai chi exercises, 101
Tax accountants, 130–31, 156
  lump-sum distributions and, 131,
    136
  See also CPAs
Tax-deferred savings plans, 7–9,
    75, 165
  employer contributions to, 8–9
  example of tax-savings, 51–52
  importance of, 74–75
  returns compared with taxable
    savings, 8
  See also 401(k)s; IRAs; Rollover
    IRAs

Tax-free gifts, 158
"Tax Highlights for U.S. Citizens
    and Residents Going Abroad"
    (IRS Publication 593), 124
Tax lawyers, 153
Taxes, 8, 85
  after retirement, 33
  income averaging and, 131–34
  on lump-sum distribution,
    131–34
  and penalties, 151
  property, 32
  on rollover IRAs, 131–32, 134–36
  on Social Security benefits, 24,
    26–27, 33
  28% bracket and variable
    annuities, 137
  when retiring abroad, 124
  See also Tax-deferred savings
    plans
Technology stocks, 48, 69
Temporary work, 156
Ten-year averaging, 132–34
10–year period-certain annuity, 168
Tenure reverse mortgage, 174
Term certain method, 151–53
Term reverse mortgage, 174
Texas, 114
Third quarter of life, 13
Thomas, Representative Bill, 95–96
Tillman, Robert, 120
Total-return funds, 67–68, 139
Transportation costs, 33
Travel expenses, 34
12b-1 fees, 66
Twentieth Century, 69

Uruguay, 122
"U.S. Tax Treaties" (IRS
    Publication 901), 124
U.S. Treasury 30–year bonds, 130
U.S. Treasury bills
  average annual rates of return, 76
U.S. Treasury notes, 59, 60–61

Utah, 117
Utilities, 32

Value funds, 48, 55–56, 59, 68
Vanguard, 69
  fund family, 139
  Retirement Planner software, 40
Variable annuities, 137–43
  fees and charges, 140, 141
  shopping for, 141–43
"Virgin" IRA, 152
Voluntary-separation packages, 42, 43
Volunteer work, 20–21

Warnings:
  company handling of rollover IRAs, 131–32

financial planners and lump-sum distributions, 130–31
IRA distribution schemes, 153
single-life annuity with life insurance policy protection, 129
Washington State, 105, 118
Widow/widower benefits, 29
Wilshire index, 70
Work prospects, 156, 166–67
Worksheets:
  How Much You Must Save, 36–39, 146–47
  How Much You Will Need for Retirement, 32–36, 160, 169, 170–71